1000 BEST

baby bargains

1000 BEST

baby bargains

KIMBERLY DANGER

SOURCEBOOKS, INC.®
NAPERVILLE, ILLINOIS

Published by Sourcebooks, Inc.
P.O. Box 4410, Naperville, Illinois 60567-4410
(630) 961-3900
FAX: (630) 961-2168
www.sourcebooks.com

Library of Congress Cataloging-in-Publication Data

Danger, Kimberly.
  1000 best baby bargains / by Kimberly Danger.
     p. cm.
  Includes index.
  ISBN 1-4022-0381-0 (alk. paper)
  1. Infants' supplies--Purchasing. 2. Consumer education. I.
Title: One
thousand best baby bargains. II. Title.

  RJ61.D227 2005
  649'.122'0284—dc22

                                           2005007224

              Printed and bound in Canada
              WC   10 9 8 7 6 5 4 3 2 1

TABLE OF CONTENTS

ACKNOWLEDGMENTS

This book wouldn't have been possible without the encouragement of my husband, Scott. He provided all the support I needed, not to mention countless hours of childcare while I worked to complete this book on time. I wanted to acknowledge the inspiration behind the book, my two greatest blessings, Sydney and Nicholas. They remind me every day that the best things in life are free. Thanks, too, to the readers and contributors of my website, www.Mommysavers.com.

Introduction

Congratulations! You're about to embark on the adventure we call parenthood. Awaiting your new arrival is an exciting time, but one that can be frightening for any family on a budget. A walk through a baby superstore could leave any soon-to-be parent with a serious case of sticker shock. Who ever thought such a tiny creature would need so many things?

When my daughter was born over five years ago, I stopped working full-time to become a stay-at-home mom. Money was tight, to say the least. Since I wasn't making as much money as I previously had, I decided that saving money would be my job. I read countless books and magazine articles, and visited Internet sites. I had always been thrifty by nature, but now I had to take it to a whole new level. I decided to share my knowledge with other parents by creating my own website.

Thus, in April of 2000, Mommysavers.com was born.

Mommysavers.com began with a couple dozen pages, primarily just tips on how to save money on baby items and household expenses. Now it encompasses over a thousand pages on every aspect of frugality. Our community of parents supports each other through discussion boards, shopping tips, articles, and a weekly newsletter.

This book is a collection of all the best money-saving baby advice that has been shared on the website and newsletter over the last five years. With two little ones of my own and tips from hundreds of other moms, this book encompasses the best tried-and-true tips from *real* parents. Included are some great suggestions for do-it-yourself baby products, advice on what not to buy, and how to find new things for rock-bottom prices.

The good news is that you can raise an infant on modest means without depriving yourself or your baby of anything. While retailers would have you believe otherwise, what babies need most is love, attention, and nurturing care, all of which are free. With a little time and creativity, any parent can learn to get by on even the strictest budget. Financial struggles shouldn't get in the way of you enjoying your new little one.

Have a question or comment regarding this book? Visit the website Mommysavers.com and post a message on our discussion board.

1000 BEST

baby
bargains

Part One:

Before Your Baby Arrives

The Maternity Months

THINGS TO THINK ABOUT NOW

1. Once you're pregnant, your doctor will prescribe prenatal vitamins. Even if you have a reasonable co-pay, they can be expensive. Target and Wal-Mart both have a generic prenatal vitamin available over the counter that compares to the prescription brands. The bottle contains two hundred vitamins, about enough to get you through your entire pregnancy, and costs only about $6.

2. Pregnancy books and workout videos are great to have, but don't pay full price for them. They often wind up at secondhand stores, thrift shops, and consignment stores. Or search for them on eBay.

3. For a free book on pregnancy and your baby's first year, call State Farm Insurance at 1-888-733-8368.

4. Don't buy an expensive body pillow from a maternity store. Wal-Mart carries a full-length pillow for under $10. If you find it to be too overstuffed for your liking, just open a seam and remove some of the fiberfill.

5. Steer clear of expensive creams that say they can prevent or erase stretch marks. While they sound wonderful, they can't live up to their claims. Heredity gave you stretch marks, and no amount of cream will erase them. On the upside, stretch marks do tend to fade with time.

6. Talk to your employer about the benefits you'll receive while on maternity leave. Some offer paid leave if you qualify. Most offer short-term disability after your baby is born, which is meant to cover your salary (or a portion of it) while you are unable to work due to illness, injury, or childbirth.

7. Medicaid may pay for your prenatal care if you meet eligibility requirements. Medicaid is a health insurance program for certain individuals that is funded and administered through a state–federal partnership. To find out if you meet eligibility requirements, contact your local or county medical assistance, welfare, or social services office. www.cms.hhs.gov/medicaid

8. If your insurance doesn't fully cover your prenatal care and hospital stay, investigate using a certified nurse midwife. A certified nurse midwife is a registered nurse who has gone on to complete further training in childbirth situations and is a safe alternative to an MD as long as you have a normal pregnancy without any complications. Many women claim their birth experience is more fulfilling with a midwife, and is far less costly than using a doctor and hospital.

9. See if your hospital offers childbirth or Lamaze classes to expectant parents. Most offer these courses free of charge to parents who will be giving birth there. Not only will you be gaining valuable information, you may form lasting friendships with other couples who will be going through the stages of parenthood at the same time you are.

10. In the last month before giving birth, stock your freezer with meals you can eat when your baby arrives. Once your baby is here, you won't have much time or energy to cook. Having meals at your disposal will prevent you from spending needlessly on take-out and convenience items.

11. Start stocking up on baby items now. If money is going to be tight after your little one arrives, start buying right away. For example, buy one pack of diapers for each paycheck you receive (just be sure not to buy too many of one size). This will ease the financial strain on your family once the baby comes.

HAVE A BABY SHOWER!

12. Do have a baby shower. Don't feel guilty, even if you have to ask a friend or family member to host one for you. Most are happy to do so. People who are invited to your shower would most likely want to give you a gift anyway, and this way they get to share in the celebration of your impending arrival.

13. Don't hesitate to return unneeded items you receive at your shower. Your friends would want you to have what you wanted, and would hate to have something sit unused.

14. Be sure to register for gifts. A gift registry can serve as a guide to friends who want to buy you a gift but are unsure of your wants and needs. Most retailers will also offer you valuable coupons for baby products when you register. Having a registry also makes things easier for you when you need to return unneeded items.

15. Ignore the "suggested" list the stores provide when you register. Most encourage you to buy much more than you actually need. Talk to experienced mothers and find out what they think is really helpful and what is not.

16. Don't request theme items. Unless you want to end up with lampshades, outlet covers, and wall hangings adorned with Peter Rabbit, avoid telling friends and family which theme you've chosen. There are more practical ways to spend money.

17. If you don't need a lot of baby items or are unsure as to what you'll need, add gift cards to your registry. They will be handy to have later on as different needs arise.

18. Invite the guys, too. Invite all your friends, regardless of whether they're male or female. An outdoor grill-out or Sunday football bash may appeal to the men on your guest list. The hostess can tell them the only shopping requirement is to pick up a pack of diapers in any size.

19. Don't forget to request practical items like diapers, wipes, and formula. Even add them to your gift registry. Having these necessities on hand will free up your own money for future expenses.

20. Register for things to make your life as a parent easier. A new cordless phone, a new camera, a hand-held vacuum cleaner, or a special journal or scrapbook are all things you may wish you had after your baby arrives.

21. Wait until *after* your shower to buy baby items. Until you receive the majority of your gifts, you really don't know what you will need. It is best to wait to make any major purchases.

22. Register online. Stores like Babies "R" Us allow you to create a registry online in just minutes. Your registry can be accessed by anyone who uses the Internet or visits the store. The outlet portion of their website carries discounted baby gear, layette, feeding supplies, and clothing at up to 50 percent off.

WHEN THE BIG DAY COMES

23. Don't spend your money on expensive nightgowns or sleepwear for the hospital. The gowns the hospital provides are comfortable, great for nursing, and you won't have to worry if they get stained. Instead, purchase a robe to slip on when visitors come (if you don't have one already).

24. Call your insurance provider before entering the hospital to see exactly what will be covered in your hospital stay. Ask what supplemental pain medications and services are included with your plan, such as an anesthesiologist who administers an epidural. Some plans don't cover such things, so be sure you find out in advance.

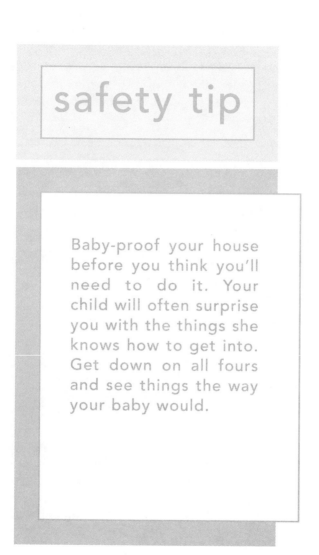

safety tip

Baby-proof your house before you think you'll need to do it. Your child will often surprise you with the things she knows how to get into. Get down on all fours and see things the way your baby would.

25. Bring your baby book to the hospital. The nurses can stamp your baby's footprints and handprints in it when they stamp them for the birth certificate. This saves you time and the cost of buying an ink kit to do it yourself later.

26. When you go to the hospital, make sure you bring along your own ibuprofen or aspirin to help manage the pain after birth. Hospitals sometimes charge quadruple the cost for most medications, so you can save a lot of money by bringing your own.

27. Refuse anything you don't need. Remember that you're most likely paying for each pill, nursing pad, and sanitary item that the nurses give you.

28. Be sure to pack a prepaid phone card in your bag or purse to go to the hospital. Once your bundle of joy arrives, you'll want to spread the news! Avoid long distance and additional cell phone charges by using a phone card.

29. Bring along some snacks for you and your guests in the hospital. Vending machines are usually available, but can be unhealthy and cost a lot of money.

30. Skip the photographs of your newborn that the hospital sells. These photos are very pricey (most packages start at $40) and are typically taken by a nurse, not a professional photographer. Instead, take your own photos in the hospital and wait two weeks to have a professional portrait taken at a studio. In a couple weeks, your baby will have much more character and you'll pay a fraction of the cost of the hospital pictures. Plus, you'll have your choice of backgrounds and props.

31. If you're not going to be nursing your baby, ask the hospital for more formula. Your nurses are usually happy to give you more samples before you leave.

32. Take the goodies in your baby's bassinet at the hospital along home with you. Your insurance company gets billed for them regardless of whether you take them home or not. This goes for toiletries for mom as well (the witch hazel pads, peri-bottle, and toothpaste are yours to take).

33. Before you leave the hospital, find out if there is a toll-free number or hotline available for you to call with any medical questions. It may save you an unnecessary trip to the emergency room with your baby in the middle of the night.

34. Be sure to review your bill carefully once it arrives to make sure you aren't charged for any goods or services you didn't receive. If you do find an error in your invoice, notify your insurance provider right away. Keep detailed documentation of any dealings you have with insurance companies and write down the names of medical and billing personnel with whom you speak.

35. Make your own Tucks pads by soaking a maxi-pad in witch hazel. You can even put them in the freezer. (It won't freeze because witch hazel contains alcohol.) The coolness is comforting to tender episiotomy sutures.

36. Save your sheets by placing a thin beach towel on your side of the bed. Postpartum mothers are leaky creatures. Not only will your breasts leak, you will be shedding your water weight through perspiration.

2

Clothing Tips for Mom-to-Be

THE SKINNY (OR NOT-SO-SKINNY) ON MATERNITY CLOTHES

37. It isn't necessary to purchase a maternity bra. Even though they claim to fit even as you change sizes, most don't. Regular bras with a little more support will do just fine.

38. A jogging bra is an inexpensive alternative to a maternity bra. Most contain spandex, which accommodates ever-changing sizes well. Some moms even claim they are comfortable to wear to bed when their breasts are tender.

Refinishing or stripping furniture should be left up to another family member, not the expectant mom. Most chemicals used in refinishing are highly toxic and could be dangerous to you and your unborn baby.

39. Don't buy everything all at once. Start with items such as jeans, khaki pants, and basic shirts and add to your collection as needed.

40. Garage sales can be a great source for inexpensive maternity wear. If you're at a garage sale that has clothing for newborns, ask if they have maternity clothing as well. Sometimes the seller simply forgets to put it out.

41. Ask friends who have just had a baby if they're interested in selling their maternity clothing, especially if you know they're done having children. Most will be happy to help you out by finding a new home for clothing they no longer need.

42. Don't forget to look for maternity clothing in thrift shops. While selection is limited, you may find a few bargains. While you're there, also look for plus-size clothing or larger-sized clothing that can double as maternity wear.

43. Buy regular clothing in a size larger than you usually do. These pieces will be useful when you're in that not-quite-showing stage of pregnancy. This clothing will also be useful postpartum as you're losing that extra weight.

44. Look for loose-fitting dresses and jumpers to wear while you're pregnant. These styles seem to work out well as maternity wear, and can often be found on sales racks at the end of the season.

45. When you buy new pieces, make sure they match the styles and colors you typically wore before becoming pregnant. Otherwise, you'll end up spending even more money on shoes, earrings, and other accessories.

46. Avoid buying maternity clothes that are too small. When trying on pieces you plan on wearing through the end of your pregnancy, use a belly pillow to make sure it will still fit later on.

47. Shop wisely. When buying at maternity retailers, be sure to inquire about their return policy. Many of them have strict policies that prevent customers from returning things after 10 or 14 days of purchase.

48. eBay is a great source for maternity clothes. Look for groups or "lots" of clothing to save even more money. Be sure to note the condition of the clothes you're buying, and pay close attention to the seller's feedback rating. Ask any questions about sizing prior to placing your bid because you won't be able to try them on before buying.

49. Check department stores such as Kohl's, Sears, JCPenney, and Mervyn's. These stores offer regular-priced maternity clothing, but you can occasionally find some great bargains on their clearance racks.

50. Target offers some of the best bargains out there for maternity apparel. They even offer designs by Liz Lange (designer to fashion-conscious Hollywood moms). While their regular prices are great (hardly anything over $25), their sales are even better. It's not uncommon to find bargains marked down 30, 50, or even 75 percent on a regular basis. Their maternity clearance is not located in a separate section, so be prepared to look through the regular ladies' clearance racks.

51. Wal-Mart offers maternity wear at reasonable prices. They have a good selection of basics like jeans and tees. Hardly anything is over $20, and they also offer clearance merchandise.

52. If you have a formal occasion, consider renting a dress. Look in your yellow pages or do a search online to see if there are stores in your area that rent maternity apparel.

53. Shop factory outlets. For a listing of maternity outlets in your state or area, go online. Sites like www.outletbound.com will be able to tell you which stores are in your vicinity.

54. Motherhood Maternity, a popular boutique for maternity wear, has over 100 outlet stores around the United States. While their outlet prices are comparable to their regular stores, you can often find great deals in the back of the store on their clearance racks.

55. While Gap doesn't stock maternity apparel in each of their regular stores, most of their outlet stores offer a very small selection of maternity clothing. Look in the rear of the store near the baby/layette department. You are likely to find a couple styles of pants and/or blouses available at outlet pricing.

56. While only select Old Navy stores offer maternity clothing in-store, they sometimes stock returns from their online maternity department. Check the clearance racks of their bricks-and-mortar stores for any maternity clothing that has been returned.

BUYING YOUR MATERNITY CLOTHES ONLINE— INEXPENSIVELY

57. Babystyle.com offers maternity wear for the fashion-conscious mom. Many of their designs are on the dressy side and appeal to working moms, but they do offer casual wear as well. The best bargains can be found in their outlet. Search by markdown percentage (up to 70 percent) to find the best deals.

58. Landsend.com has maternity wear, but you have to really search for it. They don't have maternity listed as a separate category in their site directory. However, when you click on the "Overstocks" tab and enter "Maternity" in their search box, you almost always get a page or so of markdowns to browse. Most are substantially reduced.

59. Maternitymall.com is a portal for several maternity clothing brands offering their goods online. Stores like Motherhood, A Pea in the Pod, and Mimi Maternity can all be accessed. Click on the "Sale" tabs to view clearance merchandise at up to 75 percent off.

60. Do a search of other retailers that offer maternity apparel online. Some include: www.onehotmama.com—
   Click on "Hot Deals" to save 50 percent or more.
www.momshop.com—
   Click on "Clearance" to browse their markdowns.
www.maternityapparel.com—
   Click on "Sale Pages" or "Below Wholesale" for the best bargains.
www.maternity4less.com—
   Click on their "Belly Bargains" page for sale items.

61. Try a bartering board for maternity clothing. Mommysavers.com has a bartering board where parents can trade goods and services without money changing hands.

safety tip

While today's latex paints are safer than lead-based paints of a generation ago, you should still steer clear of inhaling noxious paint fumes while pregnant. Enlist the help of your spouse, another family member or friend when it comes to painting your nursery.

62. Retailers like Gap offer a considerable selection of maternity clothing online comparable to the quality and price of their non-maternity apparel. Many moms-to-be like it because the styles compare to what they would be wearing if they weren't pregnant. The best bargains can be found online by clicking on the "sale" or "clearance" tabs. It's not uncommon to find final markdowns for $6.97 each.

63. Old Navy, Gap's lower-priced counterpart, also offers maternity clothes online and has a "bargains" section of their website devoted to maternity wear.

64. Buy with online coupons to save even more money. You can find the best bargains by combining clearance items with free shipping and online coupon codes. Stores like Old Navy, Gap, and BabyStyle frequently offer codes good for free shipping or another specified discount. For a listing of coupon codes, visit the website Mommysavers.com.

65. Consignment stores may also carry maternity wear. Consult your yellow pages to see if there are any consignment stores in your area and give them a call before stopping by.

66. Stores that sell used baby items, such as Once Upon a Child, may also stock maternity clothing. Call before you go, as not all of their locations carry maternity wear. For a listing of stores in your area, visit their website. www.ouac.com

67. If you shop for maternity clothes at Old Navy, Gap, or other well-known national retailers, look for gift cards on eBay. You can frequently find gift cards for 20 percent off of their face value. For example, you may be able to purchase a $100 gift card for $80. Be sure to read the description carefully and check the seller's feedback rating before making your purchase.

GETTING THE MOST OUT OF YOUR REGULAR CLOTHING

68. Turn your regular pants into maternity pants by safety-pinning a strip of elastic onto the waistband (a hair elastic also works well secured through the buttonhole of your jeans and hooked onto the button). Your maternity tops should be long enough to cover the fly area anyway, and no one will ever know the difference. The solution isn't permanent, so you can go back to wearing your pants normally after baby is born.

69. To save money on maternity clothing, raid your husband's closet (assuming, of course, that he's bigger than you are). Loose-fitting items such as T-shirts, sweaters, and sweatshirts will look just fine, even if you have to push up the sleeves. Adding feminine accessories such as necklaces or scarves will take off the masculine edge.

70. Drawstring pants work well as maternity wear. They can be adjusted as you grow and can be used after your baby is born when you're trying to shed extra pounds.

71. Overalls and shortalls work well as maternity wear. You can pair them with your regular, nonmaternity shirts. Even if the shirts don't provide enough tummy coverage, the overalls will minimize skin exposure.

72. Avoid having to buy maternity panty hose by wearing your regular hose and rolling or folding down the waist to just under your belly, or wear longer dresses and pantsuits with thigh-high or knee-high hose.

73. Look for low-rise jeans instead of maternity jeans. Your ever-expanding belly won't be constrained by a waistband, allowing room for growth.

74. Maternity underwear isn't necessary. Bikini underwear works well because it rests under your belly, not over it. Save your money for attractive lingerie when you're not pregnant anymore.

75. Do invest in accessories you can wear later. A new pair of earrings, a scarf, or a fun handbag can help make you feel more put together when your wardrobe isn't what it used to be.

76. Many people's feet swell during pregnancy, especially during the hot summer months. Instead of purchasing an expensive pair of shoes, buy flip-flops or other slip-ons. Not only are they less expensive, they allow more room for your feet to expand.

3

Bargains for Multiple Bundles

TWINS, TRIPLETS, AND MORE

77. Don't fall into the trap of buying two of everything. You will need two of certain items (car seats, for example) but not items like toys. Be sure to think through each purchase to determine whether or not you'll really need more than one.

78. Join a twins or multiples group (or start one yourself). Not only will the other parents provide valuable moral support, you'll get a lot of great ideas on saving money from your network of parents.

79. Check into which multiples groups in your area have rummage sales. Some offer early shopping to mothers of multiples.

80. Instead of buying two bath seats for your tub, use two inexpensive laundry baskets. The baskets fit well in the tub, one behind or aside the other, and babies are more contained. When they're ready for the full tub, you can use the baskets for laundry.

81. You may not need two cribs. Many parents of twins find that their babies not only enjoy sharing a crib, but prefer it. You may be wise to wait until your babies are older to see if you'll need to buy an additional crib.

82. Feed multiples with one bowl and one spoon if no one is sick. This is so much easier than feeding with two spoons and two bowls.

83. A hanging shoe bag hung inside your babies' closet is a great alternative to a dresser. Put two outfits in each slot, making getting dressed in the morning much easier.

84. Save time when making large batches of formula by using a pitcher. Make enough for a day's supply, and either store the pitcher in the fridge or pour it directly into bottles.

FREEBIES FOR MULTIPLES!

85. Beechnut Food Corporation will send parents of multiples coupons if you call their toll-free number. 1-800-523-6633

86. Call Evenflo Products for information on receiving multiples starter kits, which include diaper pail liners, bibs, and coupons for other products. 1-800-356-BABY

87. Gerber also has a multiple-birth program. Contact them at 1-800-4-GERBER for baby food, coupons, spoons, and the like.

88. Johnson & Johnson offers free gifts to parents of multiples. 1-800-526-3967

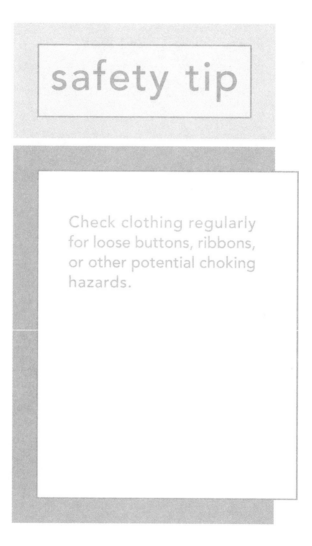

safety tip

Check clothing regularly for loose buttons, ribbons, or other potential choking hazards.

89. Huggies offers coupons for diapers and wipes to parents of multiples. You'll need to provide copies of the birth certificates and mail them to:

U.S. Requests:
Kimberly-Clark Corporation
Department QMB
PO Box 2020
Neenah, WI 54957-2020

Canadian Requests:
Kimberly-Clark, Inc.
Department QMB
50 Burnhamthorpe Road West
Mississauga, ON L5B 3Y5

90. JCPenney's portrait studio offers a multiple birth program. Complete the online form to receive a pair of portrait sitting coupons for your twins.
www.jcpenneyportraits.com/multiples

91. Babies "R" Us offers a 10 percent discount to parents of multiples when they purchase two or more of the same products in the same order. The discount pertains to the following categories only: furniture, bedding sets, and baby gear. For more details, visit your nearest Babies "R" Us store.

92. Parents of twins or triplets can receive a special assortment of Ocean Spray product coupons in the multiple-birth program. Send a copy of proof of birth of your multiples to:

Ocean Spray Cranberries, Inc.
One Ocean Spray Drive
Lakeville-Middleboro, MA 02349

93. Contact Playtex Products for a $7.00 rebate on the purchase of a Diaper Genie. Either call 1-800-222-0453 or mail your request to:

Playtex Products
20 Troy Road
Whittany, NJ 07981

94. The Drypers Corporation will send you a coupon for a free package of diapers for each baby. 1-360-693-6688.

95. Call the makers of Enfamil at 1-800-222-9123 for information on receiving a free case of formula for your twins, triplets, or quads.

96. Playtex will send the parents of multiples information on receiving bottles, liners, and pacifiers, so call 1-800-222-0453.

97. Call Proctor and Gamble, the makers of Pampers and Luvs, at 1-800-543-0480 to receive a package of free diapers for each baby.

98. Carter's has a free clothing program available to parents of triplets. Send copies of your children's birth certificates (please note the gender of each child) to:

The William Carter Company
Attn: Multiple Birth Program
224 North Hill Street
Griffin, CA 30223

99. OshKosh B'Gosh gives a 10 percent discount on all products sold in their stores if you have twins, triplets, or other multiples, including sale and clearance items. Just tell the cashier that you are a parent of multiples when you check out.

100. The First Years has a multiple-birth program open to parents of twins, triplets, or other multiples. You'll receive free gifts from their current product lines. Contents may vary, but past gifts have included bibs, rattles, teethers, and toys. Just send photocopies of your children's birth certificates to:

The First Years
Attn: Multiple Birth Program
One Kiddie Drive
Avon, MA 02322

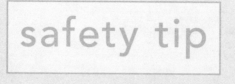

safety tip

Any baby showing signs of dehydration should be under the care of a physician. Symptoms include crying with no tears, decreased urination (less than 4 wet diapers in 24 hours) dry mouth and tongue, sunken eyes, grayish skin, and a sunken fontanel (soft spot) on baby's head.

Part Two:

Feeding Your
Newborn Baby

4

Breast-Feeding

YOUR OWN MILK IS HEALTHY—AND FREE

101. Breast-feed if you can. It is much cheaper than formula (which can run up to $1000/year) and is healthier for your baby. Plus, breast milk is always ready and available at the perfect temperature. It contains all the vitamins and minerals that your baby needs and provides an irreplaceable bonding experience for mother and child.

102. Breast-feeding also helps save on health-care expenses. Studies show breast-fed babies are less likely to suffer from allergies, asthma, ear infections, gastroenteritis, and juvenile diabetes. This means they need fewer doctor visits and are hospitalized less often than their formula-fed counterparts. For working mothers, that means an added savings of less time lost on the job.

103. Breast-feeding provides health benefits for mom, too. Studies show that mothers who breast-feed are less likely to suffer from postpartum depression and certain forms of cancer. It also helps moms get the baby weight off faster.

104. By exclusively breast-feeding, chances are you won't have a period until you've weaned your baby. Not only do you save money on formula, you also don't have to buy feminine hygiene products.

105. If you have trouble breast-feeding, consult a lactation nurse. Most breast-feeding problems are common and can be worked through. Many hospitals offer this service for free. If a lactation consultant isn't available to you, contact the La Leche League. Check your phone book to see if your hometown has a local branch, or visit their website. www.lalecheleague.org.

106. Most moms experience a period where demand for milk exceeds supply. This can be remedied by drinking water, eating products made of oats, and pumping in between feedings to stimulate supply. Check with your lactation consultant or La Leche League for other methods of improving milk supply.

107. It's not too late! Most women assume that if they didn't start nursing right away or if they allowed their milk to dry up they can't go back. In some cases, relactation is a possibility. Don't rule it out, especially if your baby develops problems such as reflux, for which you would have to purchase expensive formulas. Consult your doctor or lactation nurse to see if relactation is a possibility for you.

108. It's not all-or-nothing. Even nursing your baby once or twice a day will save money on formula. Your body will adapt to whatever feeding schedule you and your baby establish.

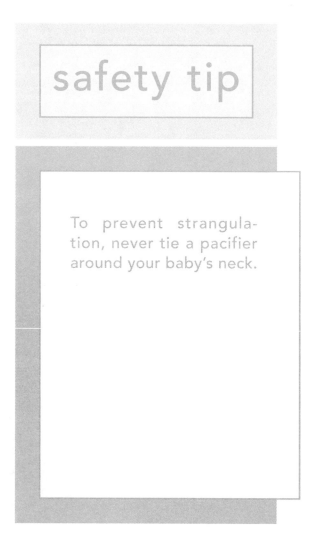

safety tip

To prevent strangulation, never tie a pacifier around your baby's neck.

NURSING APPAREL

109. Invest in at least two or three good nursing bras if you plan on breast-feeding more than a couple months. Your breasts change shape and size through different stages of nursing, so you'll need the added support. Choose one in 100 percent cotton that isn't too tight to avoid problems like thrush and clogged milk ducts.

110. Wait until late in pregnancy (the last month, preferably) to purchase a nursing bra. At this point your breasts will be closest to the size they will be while nursing.

111. Check discount retailers for nursing bras. Both Target and Wal-Mart have inexpensive nursing bras in the $10–$12 range that hold up fairly well.

112. Search for nursing bras online. Certain sites sometimes run clearance sales, and you may find a style you like for as little as $5. Be sure to check out the sale section of Bosom Buddies. www.bosombuddies.com

113. You will find that clothing designed specifically for nursing isn't necessary. Most of your regular clothing will work just fine.

114. If you want to buy clothing that's more functional for nursing, purchase regular button-down shirts or loose-fitting blouses. If the shirt is a little loose and on the long side, there is enough material there to still keep you covered. Choose patterns in dark colors to hide leaks, spit-up, and other inevitable messes that come with nursing a baby.

115. Skip the nursing cape. Bring a blanket with you wherever you go so that you can cover up regardless of what you're wearing. If you're on the go, places like fitting rooms, bathrooms, or even your car can give you the privacy you crave while nursing.

116. Men's button-down shirts work well for nursing. Borrow some from your husband's closet.

117. If you're more comfortable wearing nursing apparel, buy some inexpensive tees or turtlenecks to wear under sweaters or blouses. Purchase them on clearance and cut slits in them yourself. (you need to stitch around the openings so it won't unravel over time). You can also wear the T-shirts under sweaters, which keeps you completely covered, or you can wear a cardigan sweater or a jacket. You can also nurse in a regular shirt and easily stay covered up.

118. Disposable breast pads are convenient, but costly. Instead, purchase a few pairs of machine-washable cotton breast pads that can be used over and over again.

119. Make your own breast pads. Be sure to use fabric that is 100 percent cotton (your husband's old T-shirts work well) allowing your skin to breathe. Cut several layers of circles and stitch an X through all the layers to keep them in place. To finish, zigzag or serge the round edge.

120. Pantyliners cut in half can double as disposable breast pads. They are just as absorbent but cost much less.

121. A disposable diaper cut into circles can also be used as a breast pad. This is a great way to use up diapers your baby has outgrown.

122. If you sew, look for patterns for nursing apparel and make a few tops. Elizabeth Lee Designs features patterns designed especially for the breast-feeding mom. www.elizabethlee.com

123. A baby can nurse comfortably and discreetly in a baby sling. While a new one may cost up to $40, it may be worth the investment, or Elizabeth Lee Designs sells a pattern to make one yourself. www.elizabethlee.com

124. Look on eBay for nursing apparel. You may find gently used or even new nursing items at great savings.

125. Sites that sell maternity clothing usually offer nursing apparel as well. Search the bargain areas of their websites to find the best deals.
www.onehotmama.com—
    Click on "Hot Deals" to save 50 percent or more.
www.momshop.com—
    Click on "Clearance" to browse their markdowns.
www.maternityapparel.com—
    Click on "Sale Pages" or "Below Wholesale" for the best bargains.

126. Switch to pajamas. It's much easier to pull up a pajama top than unbutton a nightgown in the middle of the night. If you are used to wearing nightgowns and can't make the switch, take a couple of your older ones and cut slits in the side seams for nursing. You can stitch them back up when you're done nursing, or simply toss them out.

safety tip

The safest place for your baby's car seat is in the backseat. Placing it in the middle of the seat will help protect baby in the event of a side-impact collision. Be sure to use it in the rear-facing position until baby is twelve months of age.

BREAST MILK STORAGE, PUMPS, AND ACCESSORIES

127. C-shaped nursing pillows, such as the Boppy, are nice but not necessary. Simply propping your arms up on a couple pillows should do the trick nicely. If you decide you want a Boppy, search for one at a thrift store, consignment store, eBay, or even make your own.

128. Nursing stools elevate your lap to help comfortably position you and your baby for nursing. However, their slanted design makes them impractical for use after you're no longer nursing. Instead, purchase a sturdy wooden step stool your child can use later.

129. An electric breast pump can be expensive, but it's worth the money. The Medela Pump In Style model is highly recommended, which can retail for up to $300. It is an electric-powered double pump that allows you to empty both breasts quickly and at the same time. Manual or battery-operated breast pumps are much cheaper, but they are extremely time-consuming and don't work nearly as well.

130. If you purchase your pump through a hospital, your insurance provider may cover part of the cost. Medicaid allows for a free breast pump for moms who need to go back to work or school.

131. Borrow a pump from a friend or look for a good used pump at a consignment store or on eBay. Don't be squeamish about buying a used pump. Purchase the pump only, and buy new attachments for it. The breast milk never touches the pump itself anyway.

132. If you're set on buying a new pump, buy across the border. Kidalog, a Canadian company, offers the Medela Pump in Style for $264.95 Canadian. This translates to about $194 U.S. dollars, saving you nearly $70 dollars! www.kidalog.com

133. eBay is also a source for new, high-quality breast pumps. Be sure to look for a reputable seller with a high feedback rating.

134. Renting is expensive. Most hospitals will rent breast pumps for about $30/month. If you're going to be breast-feeding for more than a couple months it is more economical to buy a new pump and resell it when you're done, especially if you'll be using it for more than one child.

135. Most breast-feeding moms fall victim to cracked or sore nipples, especially when they first start nursing. Lanolin creams for dry and cracked nipples work well, but are extremely expensive. Breast milk itself is a natural healing agent. Rub a little milk on your nipples and allow to air-dry for ten minutes.

136. If you do develop clogged milk ducts, try a warm compress. You don't have to purchase a hot water bottle or heating pad. Taking a hot shower works well, as does inserting a warm tea bag under your breast pad. Even soaking a clean diaper in warm water and using it as a hot compress works well.

137. It isn't necessary to purchase special breast milk storage bags or containers. Pour breast milk into ice cube trays and freeze. When frozen, pop them out and store in one-gallon freezer bags.

138. You can also pour your milk directly into smaller-sized Ziploc bags. This method makes thawing and using it a little easier. When it comes time to use, thaw and snip the corner off one side of the bag. Now you can pour the milk right into the bottle!

139. Contact Lansinoh for a sample of their pure lanolin breast cream. Lansinoh cream soothes sore, cracked nipples and is safe for your baby as well. Call 1-800-292-4794 or email resheda@lansinoh.com.

5

Formula, Milk, and Bottles

IF YOU CHOOSE FORMULA

140. If you're going to be using formula instead of breast-feeding, buy the powdered kind. While it may be handier, the ready-to-feed varieties cost about double the price per ounce.

141. Join formula manufacturers' mailing lists to receive valuable offers by mail. Not only will you receive free samples, but you will also get coupons and retail checks good for purchasing full cans of formula.

142. When you enroll in Similac's Welcome Addition Club, you'll receive newsletters containing pregnancy and parenting advice, tips, and special offers that may include money-saving discounts, formula samples, or other gifts. www.welcomeaddition.com

143. Enroll in the Enfamil Family Beginnings Club to receive lots of freebies and offers such as a diaper bag and changing pad, coupons for portrait sittings, and retail checks for formula. www.enfamil.com

144. Sign up for a free subscription to Nestle's Very Best Baby Club. You'll receive information on stages of feeding your baby goes through, recipes, and valuable retail checks for their formula. www.verybestbaby.com

145. Store Brand Formulas is run by Wyeth, who manufactures store-brand formulas packaged under a variety of store labels. Find nutritional comparisons and information on where to find store-brand formulas in your area. www.storebrandformulas.com

146. Baby Basic. For a free 16-ounce can of Baby Basic formula, call 1-800-864-9652. Limit one free can per household.

147. Sign up to receive free coupons from all the formula manufacturers, even if your baby favors one particular brand. You can always trade your coupons with other moms. Look online to find coupon-trading communities. Try the Mommysavers.com bartering board to trade with other moms.

148. Store-brand formulas such as Parent's Choice from Wal-Mart are just as nutritionally sound as name-brand formulas. By law, all formula manufacturers have to adhere to the same FDA guidelines. By purchasing a cheaper brand, you don't have to worry that you're skimping on nutrition.

149. Formulas containing DHA (docosahexaenoic acid) and ARA (arachidonic acid) cost more than those that don't. There is no research to support their benefits, so there's no need to splurge for formulas that contain them.

150. If you're not going to be using it right away, refrigerate your formula immediately after mixing it. If you haven't used it within two days, toss it out. You should also dispose of any room-temperature formula that has been sitting for over an hour. If you're going to be taking it with you, keep it in an insulated bag with a cool pack.

safety tip

Never put a small infant in a jogging stroller or bike trailer. The jarring motion puts added strain on baby's developing spine. Wait until your baby is strong enough to sit upright by himself and hold his head steady, or until he's one year old. Always make sure your child wears a helmet in a jogging stroller.

151. When deciding which can of formula to buy, figure the cost per ounce of the formula when it's prepared, not the cost per ounce of the powder itself. Cans and scoop sizes can vary, making it difficult to compare prices directly.

152. Prices for formula may vary within the same chain. For example, one discount retailer may sell its Similac for one price while another store 20 miles away sells it for a bit more. Call stores in your area to compare prices.

153. Ask your pediatrician for formula samples when you're at your well-baby checkup. Most offices have an abundance of samples and are happy to share them with you if you ask.

154. Formula coupons can be purchased off eBay for about half of their face value. This is especially helpful if your baby requires a special type of formula such as Alimentum or Nutramigen. Be sure to check the seller's feedback rating and find out what the expiration date of the coupon is.

155. Cans of formula itself are auctioned on eBay, too. Before bidding, make sure you know what the expiration date on the can is. Also, be sure to figure the cost of shipping in your bid.

156. Amazon.com is another not-so-well-known source for baby formula. They offer the large economy-sized cans, often at prices less than Target or Wal-Mart. As an added bonus, they often offer free shipping on qualifying orders.

157. Check the damaged section of your local grocery store for formula. You may save 25–50 percent on a can that has a little dent. Never purchase a can that has been opened.

158. Use a funnel to get the last bit of formula out of the can. There is usually enough powder left in the bottom of the can to make an extra ounce or two.

159. If your baby needs a specialized formula for medical reasons such as reflux or allergies, you can try to get your insurance provider to cover the cost. Prescriptions can be written for formulas. Be sure to ask your doctor for details.

160. If your insurance doesn't cover the cost of specialized formulas, call the manufacturer. Many of them have "helping hands" programs that provide discounts or free formula cans to families in need.

161. The biggest waste of money is "nursery water," which is promoted along with baby formula. A gallon can cost as much as $2. Don't fall victim to this marketing ploy! The water your family uses for drinking should be safe for baby as well.

162. In a pinch, formula can be made at home. However, even when made properly it is still inferior to breast milk and formula. Check with your pediatrician before introducing this to your baby.

2 12-ounce cans evaporated milk
32 ounces water (boiled and cooled)
2 tablespoons corn syrup
3 ml. Poly Vi Sol Vitamins

Mix thoroughly before serving.

163. See if you qualify for WIC. The Special Supplemental Nutrition Program for Women, Infants, and Children (better known as the WIC Program) serves to safeguard the health of low-income women, infants, and children up to age 5. Applicants must meet eligibility criteria based on income and nutritional risk. For more information and to see if you qualify, visit their website. www.fns.usda.gov/wic.

164. Travel-sized packets of formula are convenient and great to stick in your diaper bag. Just tear off the end, pour into the bottle and add water. However, they get to be expensive if you use them a lot. Instead, purchase a formula dispenser for around $3 in the baby section of Target or Wal-Mart. These little containers allow you to pour in a premeasured amount of formula into your baby's bottle mess-free.

165. Premeasure your own powdered formula into zippered snack-size baggies. It only takes a few minutes to prepare a few bags and you can carry a small pair of scissors to snip off the end to pour the powder into the baby bottle. (A small funnel may help too.)

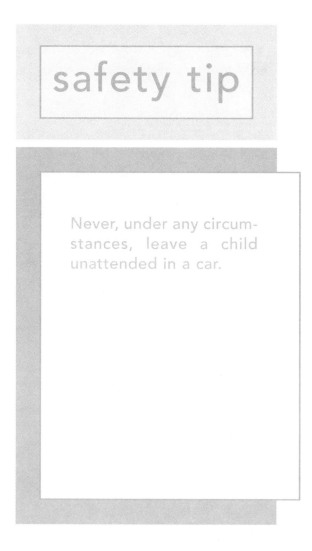

safety tip

Never, under any circumstances, leave a child unattended in a car.

MOVING ON TO MILK

166. Save your receipts if you stock up on formula. Unopened cans that haven't passed their expiration date can be returned to the store.

167. By age 12 months, most babies can move directly on to whole milk with their pediatrician's approval. Formulas designed for older babies or toddlers are costly and unnecessary.

168. If you have unopened cans of formula you can't use, consider donating them to a food shelf. Not only will you be doing something to help others, you can claim your donation as a tax deduction (be sure to ask for a receipt).

169. Don't throw away partially opened cans of formula. Instead, use the leftover formula in cooking or as a coffee creamer.

BEST BETS ON BABY BOTTLES

170. Try inexpensive baby bottles first before buying more expensive brands. They often work just as well or even better than premium bottles. Some can even be found at your Dollar Store.

171. Skip the small four-ounce bottles. It won't be long before you'll be needing the bigger ones anyway. Purchase bottles that hold eight to twelve ounces of milk, even if your baby doesn't consume that much in the beginning.

172. Use vinegar to remove water deposits on your baby bottles. Add a couple cups of white vinegar to a pot of water, and boil for about 10 minutes.

173. Don't buy those cute bottles shaped like teddy bears or puppies. Their little nooks and crannies make them extremely hard to clean, and you will most likely end up having to throw them away much sooner than regular bottles.

safety tip

Block off your fireplace. A brick hearth can produce some nasty bumps and bruises. Make sure all playthings are kept away from the fireplace and remove any fireplace tools or matches from your baby's reach.

174. Marketers would have you believe that silicone nipples are vastly superior to rubber ones. While they do last longer, it is recommended that nipples be thrown out after six months of use anyway, and rubber will definitely hold up that long.

175. Avoid bottles that come with disposable liners. Your initial investment may not be that much, but they become terribly expensive when you figure the cost of buying liners for a year or more. If your baby is colicky, you should still be able to use regular bottles. As long as you hold the bottle correctly (holding the bottom of the bottle up all the way to eliminate bubbles) your baby shouldn't get bubbles in her tummy.

176. Another alternative to bottles with liners is the Dr. Brown bottle. It uses a patented system to reduce air bubbles and simulate a natural flow, making it ideal for colicky babies. Dr. Brown Bottles are a little bit more expensive than regular bottles, but since they have no disposable parts, they are less costly in the long run.

177. Skip the bottle sterilizer. Running your bottles through the dishwasher should be sufficient to get them clean. If you notice any type of buildup in the bottle or nipple, simply boil them in a large pot of water to kill any bacteria.

178. Place nipples and tops of your bottles in a basket in your dishwasher so that they don't fall out and get burned by the heating element. You can make your own basket by using two green berry baskets from the produce department and attaching them with a twist-tie.

179. If you're a breast-feeding mom, skip the bottle stage when weaning your child. Most babies can go straight to a spill-proof cup by about six months, saving the expense of bottles. By doing so, you're also avoiding the difficulty some parents experience when taking their child's bottle away.

180. Try a new paintbrush to clean your bottle's nipples. It works just as well as a nipple brush in getting to those hard-to-reach places, and costs much less.

181. When your baby gets a little older, you'll want to get nipples that have larger holes to allow for a faster flow. Enlarge the ones you have already by inserting a toothpick in the nipple and boiling it for a few minutes, or insert a cooled sewing needle that has been sterilized by heating it with a match.

182. Don't use your microwave to warm up baby's bottle. Uneven heating can cause hot spots to form in the milk, putting your baby at risk for burning his mouth. Also, a microwave can break down essential nutrients.

183. Generic pacifiers can often be found in packages of two or three at your dollar store. They are similar to the orthodontic latex style at a fraction of the price.

184. Pacifiers are inexpensive enough to replace whenever needed, so if the nipple on a pacifier is cracked, throw it away. Pieces of the pacifier could come loose and lodge in your baby's throat.

185. Skip the bottle warmer. Simply place the bottle in a bowl of warm water for a couple minutes to heat it through. Shake vigorously to make sure it is evenly heated before offering it to your baby.

186. Your coffee pot works well as a bottle warmer. Use it to keep water warm, then place your bottle in the carafe. Within a couple of minutes, the milk will be heated through.

187. A Crock-Pot filled with water and set on low can substitute for a bottle warmer. Just mix the formula and water into the bottle and place in the Crock-Pot. Within a couple minutes it should be warm enough for your baby.

188. For nighttime feedings, boil water in the evening and place in a thermos. Leave the thermos, formula, and clean bottle on your dresser. When you get up in the middle of the night, you'll be ready to go without having to make a trip to the kitchen.

189. Remove a bottle filled with formula from the refrigerator right before you go to bed at night. By the time you need it for a late-night feeding, it will be room temperature.

6

Open Wide, Baby

FEEDING BABY ISN'T A DINNER PARTY

190. Several companies offer disposable spill-proof cups, which can be found in the infant feeding section of most large discount stores. Even though they're marketed as disposable, they can be used over and over again. If you lose or damage one, you won't feel bad about having to throw it away.

191. Mold and mildew build up easily in spill-proof cup lids and stoppers, and their tiny crevices make them hard to keep clean. Sanitize them easily by soaking them in denture cleaner tablet solution. Use hot water to dilute the tablet and let soak overnight.

192. Create a nonslip cup by wrapping a few rubber bands around your baby's cup. With a better grip, your baby will be less likely to drop it.

193. A Frisbee turned upside down can be used as a plate for baby.

194. Coffee filters or muffin cups double as serving platters for little fingers, and can be tossed when you're through with them. Look for them in bulk at your dollar store.

195. Skip the plate when baby is learning to self-feed. Instead, place food directly on the high chair tray. Babies love to pick up the plate and drop it over the edge of the chair, which creates an even bigger mess than having no plate at all.

196. A pipe cleaner can be used to clean a sippy cup lid.

197. A cute toddler cup can be made from a honey bottle shaped like a bear. Clean the bottle thoroughly to remove any trace of honey. Then cut the spout off so that you're left with a hole about the diameter of a straw.

SUPERMARKET BABY CLUBS

198. Meijer Baby Club
www.meijer.com/babyclub

Meijer's Baby Club is open to parents and parents-to-be in Michigan, Ohio, Indiana, Kentucky, and Illinois with children up to 36 months of age. Baby Club offers are sent via email.

199. Publix Baby Club
www.publix.com/services/clubs/Clubs.do

Publix Baby Club is for parents with kids under the age of two. Benefits include a free newsletter that includes coupons for free products and various other discounts.

200. A&P Baby Bonus Club
www.apsupermarket.com/bsc_baby.asp

Baby Bonus Club members receive a $20 bonus each time their Savings Club purchases add up to $200.

201. Waldbaum's Baby Club
http://waldbaums.com/baby_club.asp

Members of the Waldbaum's Baby Bonus Savings Club receive a $20 reward each time their Savings Club purchases add up to $200.

202. ShopRite Baby Bucks
www.shoprite.com

Click on "Baby Bucks" for information on getting cash back when you buy selected baby items at ShopRite stores.

203. Tom Thumb Stork Club
http://tomthumb.com/storkclub.asp

As a member of the Stork Club you will receive up-front parking for you and your new baby.
Simply stop by their Courtesy Booth and ask for a parking permit. The permit is effective three months prior and three months after the birth of your baby.

204.
Redeem your formula checks and other baby coupons at supermarkets that offer baby bucks. In most cases you will get the full value of items in baby bucks and still receive your coupon discount.

BABY FOOD—HOMEMADE OR PARENT-MADE

205.
Skip the smallest jars of baby food. Instead, buy the large jars, which are usually more economical, and freeze the excess in ice cube trays. Just pop them out when frozen and store in a zippered freezer bag.

safety tip

Keep your pet's food out of baby's reach. Not only are tiny pieces of pet food a choking hazard, your pet may become overly protective of his food and snap or bite a child that goes too close to it.

206. Before putting those cute little jars in your grocery cart, check to make sure that they haven't passed their expiration date.

207. Taste for yourself. Before feeding anything to your baby, take a little sample to check the temperature and freshness of what you're serving.

208. Never feed your baby directly from the jar unless he will finish it in one sitting. Bacteria from saliva will make its way into the jar.

209. Be sure to check ingredients in your baby food. While certain brands may be less costly, they may contain more fillers and additives, and you would have to feed your baby more to get the same amount of nutrition.

210. Food marketed to toddlers is a waste of money. It's basically table food cut into smaller, bite-sized pieces. You can create the same thing at home by cutting your own food to accommodate your older baby or toddler.

211. Make your own baby food. Cook your vegetables, meat, and fruit, then put them in a blender or food processor and blend well. Spoon into ice cube trays to freeze. Empty the ice cubes into freezer bags and thaw as needed for each serving, or plop spoonfuls onto a sheet of wax paper on a cookie sheet and freeze.

212. When making your own baby food, freeze a few servings in plastic containers. That way, you can take them out when you're in a hurry or on-the-go.

213. Cream of Wheat is an acceptable substitute for baby cereal. Like baby cereal, it is also fortified with vitamins and iron. It is available in bulk at restaurant/bakery supply stores and warehouse stores like Sam's Club, BJ's, and Costco.

214. Instant oats pulverized in a blender makes an instant baby cereal. You can purchase the oats in bulk. Prepare it ahead of time and store it in an airtight container. When you're ready to use it, just mix with breast milk, formula, or water.

safety tip

Remove poisonous plants
from your home and keep
other plants out of baby's
reach.

215. Make your own rice cereal. Start with 1/2 cup of brown rice, pulverizing it in your blender. Bring 2 cups of water to a boil. Reduce heat and add rice. Stir briskly, and remove from the burner. Cover and let stand for ten minutes, stirring occasionally to prevent sticking and clumping.

216. If you're breast-feeding, waiting a little longer to start your baby on solid food can help you save money. Most pediatricians recommend starting solids between ages four and six months. By putting off starting solids until your baby is a closer to six months, you are saving money on baby food. Besides, your baby is getting all the nutrition he needs in your milk.

217. When your baby starts to eat table food, puree or chop up your leftovers, put them in baby food jars, and freeze. Be sure to mark the date on the jar. If you add a lot of seasoning to your foods, be sure to make baby's serving first and leave the spices out.

218. Make the switch to table food early rather than relying on jarred baby food. Gradually add more and more texture to your baby's diet, so that by 7 or 8 months your baby will be able to eat bite-sized pieces of avocado, peas, cooked carrots, and so forth. He will also have lots of fun feeding himself!

219. Peel a ripe banana and spoon-feed it to baby. This costs much less than a jar of baby food, and is virtually the same thing!

220. Buy cottage cheese (large-curd works best) and rinse in a colander. The remaining pieces are great for self-feeders.

221. Other great foods for babies ready to self-feed include berries (cut into small pieces), cooked carrots, Cheerios, fish, green beans, graham crackers, noodles, pears, peas, sweet potatoes, squash, rice, and rice cakes. Remember to cook vegetables thoroughly so they're soft.

222. Prepare cereal with very little liquid so that it has a thick, clumpy consistency. Babies that are learning to self-feed can use their fingers to pick it up.

223. If you don't have enough time to make your own baby food, buy foods marketed to adults that work for baby. Unsweetened applesauce, for example, works well for baby because it is the same consistency as baby food.

224. You can often save quite a bit by buying baby food by the case at warehouse stores like Sam's Club, Costco, and BJ's Discount Club. Even superstores like Babies "R" Us and Toys "R" Us stock baby food.

225. When buying cases of baby food, you can use more than one coupon. For example, if you have a coupon for $.50 off 8 jars, you can use three coupons on a case of 24 jars.

226. Don't buy juices for your baby in the baby food aisle. Instead, make your own using regular juice and adding water. Juices for babies are really just regular juice with a higher water concentration and a little vitamin C added. Your baby should be getting a sufficient supply of vitamin C in breast milk or formula already. Mix about 1 part water to 1 part juice. Avoid juices like orange juice (which may upset little tummies) and apple cider that is unpasteurized.

227. If your baby is partial to that thick, smooth, congealed texture baby food is famous for, add a little bit of boiled potato to his food when you puree it.

228. Buy snacks such as graham crackers, Cheerios, and animal crackers in bulk. Break down the bag to smaller bags and freeze to keep them fresh.

229. Make your own Zwieback toast. Simply cut pieces of bread into strips or squares and bake in the oven at a very low temperature (150 to 200 degrees) for 15 to 20 minutes. Dark, dense breads such as wheat and rye work best.

ONLINE COUPONS FOR BABY FOOD

230. Beech-Nut
Click on the "Special Offers" tab to see a list of current promotions and coupons. Sign up to receive their free monthly e-newsletters, which often include valuable coupons to use on Beech-Nut baby foods. www.beechnut.com

231. Gerber
Click on the "Special Offers" tab for contests, coupons, and other promotions. www.gerber.com

232. Heinz
Click on the "Special Offers" tab to see a list of current promotions and coupons. Sign up to receive their free monthly e-newsletters, which include feeding information and coupons. Their rewards program lets you save UPC points redeemable for baby toys from companies like Little Tikes. (Some of their programs are limited to Canadian residents only). www.heinzbaby.com

233. Earth's Best
Click on their "Promotions and Offers" tab for coupons, UPC redemption programs, and links to other special offers.
http://earthsbest.com/

FANCY BIBS GET DIRTY, TOO

234. You can make your own baby bibs inexpensively by purchasing kids' T-shirts or sweatshirts secondhand. Leaving the front and its design, cut off the sleeves and the back. Finish the edges using a zigzag stitch or with a serger.

235. Don't bother with fancy burp cloths. Get a pack of old-fashioned cloth diapers, which are great for burping and spitting up on, and are also great as rags when you are done with them! Or simply use a dishtowel.

236. Make your own bib by taking a cloth napkin or kitchen towel and securing the ends together behind baby's neck with a pin (the kind used with cloth diapers) or a mitten clip. Keep a safety pin in your diaper bag for this purpose in case you forget to pack a bib.

237. An old bandana or scarf loosely tied behind baby's neck also doubles as a bib. A men's handkerchief or a ladies' scarf can be used for this purpose as well.

238. Another great bib can be made from a dishtowel. Cut a hole for the neck in the back 1/3 of the towel, and sew on some ribbing (or the neckline of an old T-shirt). These bibs slide easily over a baby's head and are big enough to provide complete coverage.

239. Beech-Nut offers a free bib to parents at www.beechnut.com/bib.

240. A frozen bagel works well as a teether for your baby. The cold feels great on his gums, and the bagel is easy to hold. While baby can gnaw on it quite a while without making any progress, be careful that he doesn't get any bites that are big enough for him to choke on.

Part Three:

Baby's Health
and Hygiene

7

Diapering Your New Bundle

DISPOSABLE DIAPERS

241. Store-brand diapers such as Target Brand Premium Diapers and White Cloud from Wal-Mart are just as absorbent as premium diapers and cost about $.10 per diaper less. The savings can add up to as much as $30 per month.

242. Buy diapers in bulk. As a general rule, the larger the package the lower the price per unit. Those big boxes may be harder to lug home, but they'll end up saving you money.

243. Check warehouse stores like Costco and Sam's Club for diapers. Most offer cases of premium diaper brands at a substantial discount. Don't forget to bring your coupons along for even more savings.

244. If you're using coupons, it is best to get the smallest size package available. For example, $2 off a $6 package yields a higher percentage savings than $2 off a $16 package.

245. Check Amazon.com for diapers. They frequently run sales on Pampers and Huggies and offer free shipping if you spend a certain amount.

246. Visit the Diapers 4 Less website to compare prices on diapers. Because customers buy in bulk, they can offer their diapers at a discount. www.diapers4less.com

247. Combining manufacturer's coupons and in-store sales can bring the cost of premium diapers to less than that of store brands, especially if your local grocer doubles coupons.

248. Buy the smallest size diaper your baby can fit into comfortably. While diaper packs cost the same, the larger sizes have fewer diapers inside each package. Therefore, larger diapers of the same brand are more costly.

249. If the diaper brand you are using is leaking, it can be a sign that you need to go up a size rather than switching to a more expensive brand.

250. Keep a roll of duct tape near your changing station to use when tabs get ripped off baby's diaper or no longer stick.

251. If your child has a tendency to soak through his diaper overnight, try placing a maxi pad inside the diaper rather than double-diapering him.

252. Visit the Huggies website for printable coupons and information on special offers and promotions. www.huggies.com

253. Visit the Goodnites website and find coupons in their "Special Offers" section. www.goodnites.com

254. Register for Pampers' Parent Pages newsletter and you will receive samples and coupons for Pampers products. www.pampers.com

255. To receive a sample package containing 3 Stork's Choice premium disposable diapers or 2 Stork's Choice premium training pants in the size of your choice, use the link below and click "Order Sample Pack." There is a small shipping charge. www.storkschoice.com

256. Don't stock up on diapers if your baby is nearing the next size. You don't want to be stuck with a half-used package.

257. Diapers can occasionally be found at thrift stores like Goodwill and the Salvation Army. Stores often donate packs that have been opened or damaged in some way, or parents will donate partial packs when their kids outgrow a certain size.

258. Use the big boxes/cartons that diapers come in to store outgrown baby clothes. The boxes are already marked according to size, so you'll know what size the clothes are.

safety tip

Keep emergency numbers handy and plainly visible. Make sure anyone who comes into your home to take care of your child knows where important phone numbers are.

259. Coupons for diapers and wipes can also be found on eBay. Search for keywords according to your favorite brand. Make sure you check the seller's feedback rating and find out what the expiration dates are before placing your bid.

260. If you do use premium diaper brands, ask your friends and family to cut coupons for you. Most are happy to help you out and don't mind taking the time to do so.

261. Join an online coupon-trading community to trade diaper coupons with other moms. Mommysavers.com has a bartering board where you can post your requests.

CLOTH DIAPERS

262. Try cloth diapers if you have time to launder them. Cloth diapers are better and easier to use than ever. Now they even come with Velcro closures and can be used with disposable liners. Using cloth rather than disposable diapers can save your family up to $25 per month.

263. If you're thinking of using cloth diapers, start small. Buy about half the diapers you think you'll need and commit to using them part-time in the beginning. You can always buy more if you decide to use them more frequently.

264. If you plan on using cloth diapers, skip the newborn size. Because your baby will outgrow them so quickly, it is usually cheaper to use disposables during this stage. Plus, cloth diapering does require a time commitment. When your baby is a newborn, you will need the extra time to rest.

265. It's not all-or-nothing. Even using cloth diapers while you're home can save money. Working moms can use cloth at home and send disposables with baby to day care.

266. While they save money in the long run, cloth diapers cost more with the initial investment. Contact diaper manufacturers to see if they would provide a trial pack or diaper sample to allow you to try them before making your investment.

267. If you're hesitant about giving cloth diapering a try because you don't want to be swamped with laundry, consider a diaper service. Most large cities have them. Using a service may still be more economical than using disposables, especially if you have more than one child in diapers.

268. Ask a laundry service what they do with their "retired" diapers. Most dispose of them or will sell them at rock-bottom prices. In most cases, they still have a lot of wear left.

269. When selecting your diapers, make sure to choose diaper service quality prefolds. This type has thick padding in the middle (Chinese prefolds are considered the best). Diapers from discount stores are less expensive but are much less absorbent.

270. If you're using prefolded diapers, they should be absorbent enough so that you don't need liners. If you're anticipating a leak, you can use an expensive thinner cloth diaper folded inside the prefolded one as a liner.

271. Shop for cloth diapers online. eBay also has a steady supply of new and gently used cloth diapers for sale.

272. Post a request for gently used cloth diapers on a bartering board. In all likelihood there's a mom out there who has just potty-trained her child and wants to give the cloth diapers to a new home. Check out Mommysavers.com's Bartering Board.

273. Diaper liners that haven't gotten too messy can be washed and reused several times. When they get dirty, just throw them away. A box of 50 liners can last several months!

274. Cut your cost even more when cloth diapering by making your own diapers. You can purchase patterns online, or you can even make your own pattern by tracing a diaper you already have. The materials required are very inexpensive. Some people even make them by recycling old receiving blankets or flannel sheets. For more information, visit the Born to Love website. www.borntolove.com

275. While diaper covers are helpful, it isn't necessary to use them all the time. If you're using a high-quality diaper and change it frequently, you should be able to get by without them. Just purchase a couple in the beginning for overnights, long car rides, and other situations where leaks may occur.

276. Choose a breathable fabric over plastic for diaper covers. Because they don't allow air to circulate, plastic diaper covers tend to keep too much moisture near baby's skin. The added moisture often leads to diaper rash. Choose diaper covers in nylon or another breathable fabric for baby to wear over his diaper to prevent leaks when needed. While nylon diaper covers are more expensive than plastic, they do last longer.

WASHING CLOTH DIAPERS

277. Fabric softener should not be used when laundering cloth diapers. It causes a waxy buildup on the diapers, reducing the absorbency and making the diapers water-repellent.

278. Vinegar is a natural fabric softener that removes all traces of detergent and ammonia (urine smell) from the diapers, lowers the pH level (which helps to prevent diaper rashes), and helps to whiten the diapers. Add a Downy ball half full of white vinegar. It will open up in the final rinse cycle.

279. Bleach can damage the fibers of your cloth diapers, so use it sparingly. Use chlorine-free bleach or Borax instead.

280. Try drying your stained diapers on the clothesline in the sun to bleach the stains. The sun will whiten them, and the fresh air will make them smell great!

281. When laundering diapers, first run them through a cold rinse cycle adding 1/2 cup of baking soda to the water. This will whiten your diapers, remove odors, and neutralize acidity levels.

282. Certain diaper rash ointments can leave gray strains on your diapers. Use a cream that does not contain any cod-liver (fish) oils and you'll avoid such stains.

283. Skip the baby powder. Most parents believe that sprinkling a little baby powder on baby's skin after a diaper change will absorb any extra moisture. All it really does is clump up when it gets damp, holding the moisture next to your baby's skin. It also poses a health risk to babies who accidentally inhale it. It's best not to use anything at all.

284. Rather than spending money on disposable changing pads, make your own out of a vinyl tablecloth. They can be cut into generous-sized rectangles and folded to fit in your diaper bag. They are still inexpensive enough to throw away when they get really messy.

DIAPER ACCESSORIES

285. Make your own baby wipes at home. It's quick and easy, and these wipes are a fraction of the cost of premium wipes.

286. Wipes Recipe #1
You'll need:
1 roll of premium brand paper towels*
2-1/4 cups of water
2 tablespoons baby bath or shampoo
1 tablespoon of baby oil

Cut the roll of paper towels in half using an electric knife. Mix all the liquid ingredients together. Put towels in a round plastic storage container and pour the liquid over the top. Let the mixture soak through for 5–10 minutes and pull out the center core. Wipes will pop up through the middle. *Note: Don't try to save money by using a cheap brand of paper towels. The towels will disintegrate.

287. Wipes Recipe #2
Instead of soaking the paper towels in a solution, keep the solution in a spray bottle and spray the paper towel or a baby washcloth when ready to use.

288. Instead of disposable baby wipes, consider using lightweight baby washcloths to wipe your baby. Not only are they reusable, you can also wipe your baby with a warm washcloth instead of a cold one.

289. Some of the softest baby wipes can be made from old receiving blankets. Simply cut them into rectangles and serge the edges with a sewing machine to keep them from fraying.

290. Skip the wipe warmer. They only hold a small amount of wipes, and by the time the wipe reaches your baby's bottom it may not even be that warm anymore. Plus, many older models have been recalled due to overheating. Instead, just holding the wipe in your hand for a minute will take the chill off. Body heat is free!

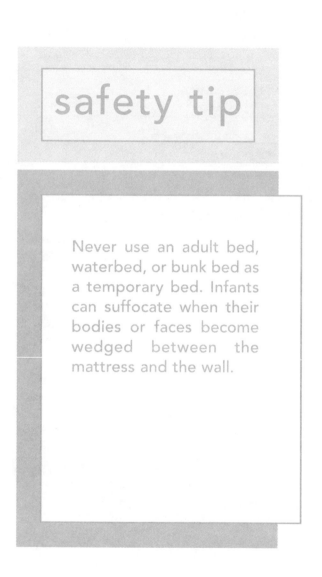

safety tip

Never use an adult bed, waterbed, or bunk bed as a temporary bed. Infants can suffocate when their bodies or faces become wedged between the mattress and the wall.

291. In most cases, store-brand wipes are just as good as premium wipes. Be sure to give the ones from Target and Wal-Mart a try. Mothers also rave about wipes from discount warehouse Costco.

292. Thick premium baby wipes can be machine-washed and reused. Soak them in the baby wipe solution mentioned above and store in the original baby wipes container.

293. Cut or tear commercial diaper wipes in half. That way, you're not using more than you actually need.

294. If you use commercial baby wipes, buy refill packs instead of purchasing a new container each time.

295. Store your container of baby wipes upside down. This helps to ensure that the top wipes will be equally as moist as the bottom ones.

296. If your wipes dry out, don't throw them away. Simply add a little water and let it soak through.

297. Skip the wipes altogether. When your baby has an especially messy diaper, take her to the tub instead of wasting 5 to 10 wipes trying to get the mess off. A handheld shower head works really well to get the mess off her bottom and is much less irritating to her skin.

298. Don't buy individual small packages of wipes for travel. Instead, put some wipes or even a wet washcloth in a Ziploc bag. When you're done, you can use the bag for diaper disposal as well.

299. If you use washcloths for wiping baby, use a color-coding system. For example, use one color of washcloths for diaper wipes and another color for bathing.

300. Consider using a regular trash can, preferably the kind with the step-on lid opener, for disposing baby's diapers. Place them in a plastic bag first. Sprinkle a little cat litter in the bottom of the can to absorb the odor.

301. The plastic bags in which newspapers are delivered are great for wrapping and disposing of dirty diapers. Bread bags and plastic grocery bags also work well.

302. Most dollar stores carry diaper-disposal bags in boxes of 100 for a dollar. They are great for using at home or packing away in your diaper bag.

303. If you buy a Diaper Genie, factor in the cost of refills. Diaper Genie disposal systems run about $25 if purchased new. However, the cost of refills ($4–$5 each) can become quite costly over time. If you decide to use a Diaper Genie, don't twist the ring after each diaper. Your refills will last much longer if you're not individually "bagging" each diaper.

304. An alternative to the bestselling Diaper Genie is the Diaper Champ by BabyTrend. While the initial investment is about the same, the Diaper Champ uses regular garbage bags as opposed to the expensive refills its competitor requires.

305. Most diaper pails are $25 if purchased new. They can often be found for $5 or less at thrift stores and garage sales and with a little bleach and warm water, they are as good as new!

306. If you do use the Diaper Genie, look for partially used refills at thrift stores or garage sales. Sometimes you can find a used Diaper Genie with the refill left inside for $5 or less. The extra Diaper Genie can be used in another room or at Grandma's house.

307. If you do buy a used Diaper Genie, make sure you buy the newer version rather than the original. The newer models in the stores today have a wider mouth, making it easier to insert an especially large diaper. The older or "original" refills are no longer on the market.

308. Swim diapers that allow baby to enjoy a pool are very expensive (most are around $.75 per diaper). Most people don't realize that they can be machine-washed and used again. Just make sure you air dry them and do not put them in the dryer.

309. Instead of buying disposable swim diapers, buy a fabric one that can be machine-washed. One fabric swim diaper costs about the same as a pack of disposables, but it can be used over and over again.

DIAPER RASH

310. Petroleum jelly is a great preventative measure if your baby is prone to diaper rash. Apply a thin coat after each diaper change, and you'll notice fewer breakouts. It also makes wiping a messy bottom much easier.

311. An even cheaper alternative to petroleum jelly is vegetable shortening. Use it just as you would any diaper rash cream, applying a thin coat with every diaper change to act as a barrier against wetness.

312. Another way to help clear up diaper rash is to wash your baby's bottom and dry it with a hairdryer. Make sure your dryer is set on the coolest setting possible, and keep it a safe distance from baby's bottom (at least six inches away).

313. If your baby has diaper rash, have him sit in a bath with a little baking soda added to the water. It quickly clears up mild rashes.

314. Keep the diaper off your baby for 15 to 30 minutes after changing him. This will allow air to circulate and promote healing.

315. Check your wipes. Commercial baby wipes containing alcohol will irritate your baby's skin and make diaper rash worse. Discontinue use until the rash has cleared up, using a warm washcloth instead.

316. Many moms swear by the antacid method. Apply a little liquid antacid such as Maalox or Mylanta with a cotton ball to baby's bottom. It will soothe baby's skin and neutralize acid.

317. Try an anti-fungal cream. Creams like those used to treat Athlete's Foot such as Lotrimin AF are also known to clear up diaper rash.

318. Mothers have been using browned flour to treat diaper rash for generations, and this old trick still works today. Place about a 1/2 cup of flour in a cast-iron skillet and heat until the flour turns completely brown. You'll want the flour as dark as possible without actually burning it. Allow it to cool completely. Place in a baby food jar with a few holes poked in the lid, and shake it on baby's bottom.

319. Less is more when it comes to diaper rash ointment and creams. Slathering on too much does more harm than good. Apply a thin coat, allowing your baby's skin to breathe.

320. In the summer, look for plain zinc oxide to use in preventing and treating diaper rash. Zinc oxide is the active ingredient in most commercial diaper rash creams, and is marketed as a sunscreen. It's usually a lot cheaper and just as effective.

8

Under-the-Weather Baby

TIPS FOR A SICK BABY

321. Visit the American Academy of Pediatrics website for information related to pediatric issues and conditions. The site includes articles written by leading health experts and recommendations supported with scientific research. www.aap.org

322. Under the Vaccines for Children program, low-income families can receive free or low-cost immunizations for their children. Every child up to 18 years of age who is enrolled in Medicaid, who lacks health insurance, or whose health insurance does not cover vaccines is eligible. For more information, visit the Center for Disease Control website. www.cdc.gov

323. Buy store-brand or generic whenever possible when buying over-the-counter medications for baby. They typically cost 50 percent less and are just as effective. Often times they are even produced by the same manufacturer, just given a different label.

324. To avoid wasting medicine, put the required dosage in a bottle nipple and push it through the hole with a clean finger. Baby won't realize it's not milk until he's taken the full dose.

325. An aloe plant is good to have around. Cut the leaves and use the aloe inside to treat bites, burns, or stings.

326. Make a soothing bath for baby with oatmeal. Put plain oatmeal in the blender and pulse till powdery. Add about 1/2 cup in the tub water for a soothing oatmeal bath. This works well for diaper rash, too.

327. Put your family's toothbrushes in the dishwasher every few days to sanitize them, preventing the spread of germs.

328. Make your own antiseptic hand gel by combining equal amounts of vodka and aloe vera gel with approximately 10 drops of fragrance oil. Stir and store in a plastic bottle. Carry it in your purse or diaper bag to use in preventing the spread of germs when soap and water isn't available.

329. Breast milk and its healing properties can be used to help children with pink eye. Just a few drops in the eye will help speed healing.

330. Small packages of ketchup and mustard can be placed in the freezer to be used as ice packs for small cuts, scrapes or abrasions.

331. Putting a couple drops of rubbing alcohol in your child's ear after swimming can help prevent swimmer's ear.

332. Make your own heating pad for baby by sewing two squares of fabric together and filling it with rice. Put the heating pad in the microwave until it is warm. It can also be used as a trivet or a stress-relieving pillow for mom.

333. Keeping your home clean can also help prevent illness. Keep countertops in your bathroom and kitchen sanitized with a disinfectant solution or spray. Launder bed linens and sheets frequently. Since babies spend a lot of time on the floor, you'll want to make sure it is as clean as possible. Have your carpets cleaned on a regular basis, and always take your shoes off at the door.

334. Wash your hands frequently. Germs and bacteria are most frequently spread by hand-to-mouth contact. Be especially careful to wash after cooking with raw meat, changing diapers, or coming into contact with any other bodily fluids. Always wash your hands before mixing formula or before feeding baby. Don't forget to wash your baby's hands, too.

CONGESTION

335. Onion makes an inexpensive natural decongestant for your baby. Cut an onion into chunks and place in a bowl. Sprinkle with a tablespoon of sugar, cover, and refrigerate for a couple of hours. The syrup that is created makes a sweet and natural decongestant. Feed baby the syrup and leave the onions behind.

336. For colds and congestion, have your baby sit in the bathroom while you run a hot shower. The warm, moist air helps loosen phlegm.

337. To alleviate sleep problems while your child is congested, have her sleep in her infant car seat. Breathing is easier with the head slightly elevated.

338. A vaporizer is effective in treating congested babies. Choose a cool-mist over a hot-steam humidifier. The hot steam poses a risk for burns or scalding.

CONSTIPATION

339. Adding a little bit of prune juice to baby's bottle can help if he's constipated. Start by adding just a couple teaspoons to the bottle and filling the bottle with milk.

340. Corn syrup can help constipated babies. A little goes a long way, however. A teaspoon added to baby's bottle should be plenty to get things moving again.

STOMACH ILLNESSES AND COLIC

341. If your child vomits on the floor, sprinkle a little cat litter over it to absorb the wetness and the smell. Sweep up after a couple minutes. Baking soda also works well.

342. Follow the "ABC" method for treating diarrhea. Apples, bananas, and cereal all help. If your child isn't old enough for solid foods, try adding a little rice water (the water rice is cooked in) to his formula.

343. Avoid giving your baby juice if he has diarrhea. It can be too acidic and will often aggravate the problem.

344. For gassy tummies, put a few ounces of warm water in a bottle. Add a pinch of sugar and mix thoroughly. Give to baby and burp well.

345. Preserve linens by placing a beach towel on baby's bedding when he's sick. A towel is easier to remove in the middle of the night than changing a sheet.

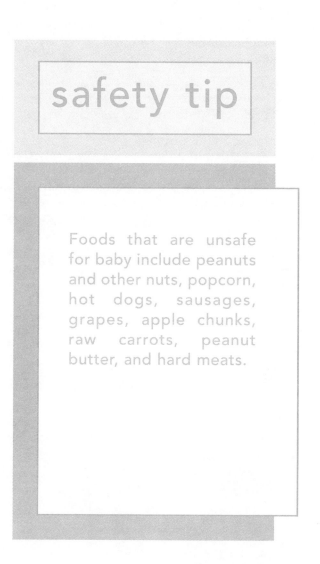

safety tip

Foods that are unsafe for baby include peanuts and other nuts, popcorn, hot dogs, sausages, grapes, apple chunks, raw carrots, peanut butter, and hard meats.

346. Make your own electrolyte solution at home by combining the following:
2 quarts water
1 teaspoon salt
1 teaspoon baking soda
1/2 cup sugar
1 packet of Kool-Aid

347. Gatorade diluted with 50 percent water is also effective in rehydrating baby and much less expensive than over-the-counter electrolyte solutions.

348. For colicky, crampy babies, put half a peppermint candy in a bottle of warm water. When it has dissolved a little, shake until the water turns pink and remove the remaining candy. The peppermint is sweet tasting and acts as an anti-gas agent. It costs much less than expensive anti-gas drops and is just as effective.

349. Avoid broccoli, asparagus, cabbage, and other gassy foods while breastfeeding. Wheat and dairy can also trigger colic in your baby. Try eating a bland diet for a while, adding more and more foods gradually so that trigger foods can be easily identified.

350. Gentle pressure applied to baby's tummy can help ease the discomfort of colic. Lay your baby face-down over your knees while you rub his back.

351. Other inexpensive ways to lull colicky babies to sleep include rocking, swinging or bouncing, swaddling, taking him for a ride in the car, or white noise.

352. Gripe Water, which can be found at your pharmacy, is a tried-and-true colic remedy.

353. The SleepTight Infant Soother is a device that attaches to your baby's crib and generates white noise similar to that of a moving car and claims to effectively reduce colic and crying. Because the SleepTight Infant Soother has been classified by the U.S. Food and Drug Administration as a medical device, it may be covered by your health insurance. Visit their website for more information. www.colic.com

SKIN CONDITIONS

354. Cradle cap is a common ailment in newborns that can be remedied easily for just pennies. Use a pea-sized amount of dandruff shampoo on your baby's scalp and brush gently with a toothbrush. The flakes should come right off.

355. Another method for removing cradle cap is to gently rub a little olive or vegetable oil onto your baby's scalp.

356. If your baby develops acne, a few drops of breast milk rubbed onto her skin may help clear it up. Breast milk contains antibacterial properties that can also help heal scratches (from baby's long fingernails) much more quickly than without it.

TEETHING

357. Over-the-counter teething gels may not be effective in alleviating your baby's pain. They are topical anesthetics that numb the surface of the gums only, but don't do much about the pain underneath. Acetaminophen or other infant pain relievers can be more effective in reducing the pain and are more long-lasting.

358. When your baby starts getting teeth, an alternative to a teething ring is a clean, damp washcloth. Babies love to chew on them, and the cool wet water feels good on their gums. You can even soak it in a little bit of apple juice and put it in the freezer.

359. Other teething remedies include: a bottle of cold water, hard teething biscuits, frozen bananas, ice chips, cold apple wedges, and cold carrot sticks. Use these methods with close parental supervision to make sure bit and pieces don't come off and become lodged in baby's throat.

360. Simply rubbing or massaging your baby's gums is also effective in treating the pain associated with teething.

SPENDING TIME IN THE SUN

361. You don't have to buy sunscreen marketed for babies. Frequently the only difference between adult and baby sunscreen is the fragrance.

362. Buy store-brand or generic sunscreen if possible. It is just as effective in blocking harmful rays as their name-brand counterparts and costs much less.

363. Use clothing (or an umbrella) to shield baby from the sun. Light-weight cotton fabric and floppy hats are great choices.

364. A sunscreen stick or sunscreen wipes are a good investment. It is often hard to get sunscreen on baby's face without it dripping and irritating eyes.

365. Babies under six months of age should not use any type of sunscreen.

9

Baby in the Bath

SAVING MONEY AT BATHTIME

366. A baby bathtub almost always can be found at a thrift store or garage sale for a couple dollars, much less than the $15–$20 it costs in retail stores. Your infant will only need it for a couple months before graduating to the big tub.

367. A large Rubbermaid container can double as a baby bath. Plus, when you're done using it as a tub, it works great to store outgrown baby clothing.

368. Consider buying an inflatable tub for your baby. It costs less than a regular baby tub and can be deflated and packed in your suitcase for travel. It also makes a fun outdoor pool for baby in the summertime.

369. Save your baby's tub when he's outgrown it. It can double as a mini-sandbox, a sensory table, or a place to store bath toys.

370. Or skip the baby bath tub altogether. Instead, bathe your baby in the kitchen sink. The sink is at a better level for a parent to bathe a child comfortably, and the spray nozzle is a nice feature to have when rinsing. Use a rubber sink mat to prevent slipping.

371. Consider giving your baby a bath while you take yours. Just make sure that the water isn't too hot. An elbow in the tub is a more reliable check than using your hand.

372. Don't buy those thin towels for baby. The towels the rest of your family uses are just fine and much more absorbent.

373. A hooded towel can be made inexpensively at home by sewing a washcloth and towel together. Fold the washcloth in half so that it looks like a rectangle. Sew one short end closed, then center the other short end of the wash cloth on the long side of the bath towel and stitch. The homemade version is much more warm and absorbent than the flimsy ones marketed for infants. Plus, as the child grows the towel serves as a great swimming cover-up.

374. When you're done using your receiving blankets, cut them into squares to use as washcloths for baby.

375. Instead of buying a non-skid liner for your bath tub, place a towel on the bottom of the tub to prevent your child from sliding around.

376. It isn't necessary to give your baby a bath more than once or twice a week. Frequent bathing not only wastes baby wash, it often leads to dry skin.

377. Don't buy a bath seat or ring designed to keep your child upright while sitting in the tub. Most have suction cups that can come unstuck, causing your baby to topple over and become pinned under the water.

safety tip

Set your hot water heater no higher than 120 degrees to avoid scalding your baby.

378. When your baby is making the transition from a baby bath tub to the big tub, use a plastic laundry basket if he is able to sit in it upright. Store bath toys in the basket when it's not in use.

379. Don't purchase a bath visor to keep water and soap out of baby's eyes. Instead, swipe a little petroleum jelly in a line on his forehead. It will deflect the water away from his face.

380. Keep all medicines out of reach of children. Keeping them in a bathroom cabinet with safety latches often isn't good enough. Keep them on a high shelf out of reach of your child. It is easy to install an inexpensive shelf if you don't already have one.

381. Keep all electrical appliances like hair dryers and curling irons out of reach. Make sure cords don't hang down, making them easy for baby to reach up and pull them down. Easily bundle your cords with a pipe cleaner or twist tie.

382. Make sure razors and other sharp objects are out of reach in the tub. Store them in a Tupperware container with a tight-fitting lid.

383. Pad the faucet with foam to avoid baby bumping her head on it.

384. Put the toilet lid down when not in use and secure with an inexpensive lid lock. Although the toilet may be fascinating to your child, he may not be able to get himself out if he falls in.

385. Never leave your child unattended while taking a bath. Invest in an inexpensive cordless phone (if you don't already have one) to take with you to the bathroom and avoid any temptation of leaving the room.

TOILETRIES

386. Contact Baby Orajel for information on teeth and gum care for infants. When you visit their website, click on the "Rebate" and "Sample" tabs for information on coupons and rebate checks by mail. www.orajel.com

387. Visit the Playtex website and sign up for their newsletter. You'll get the scoop on new products, free samples, and special offers. (Playtex manufactures Diaper Genie, Baby Magic, bottles, cups, and so on.)
www.playtexbaby.com

388. Baby bath soaps aren't necessary. Using a mild, gentle bar soap such as Dove, Aveeno, or Neutrogena works just as well and is much less expensive.

389. It isn't necessary to buy both baby shampoo and baby wash. Instead, opt for just the baby wash, which doubles as both a soap and a shampoo.

390. Contact Johnson & Johnson at 1-800-526-3967 or visit their website at www.johnsonsbaby.com for free product coupons and information on bathing your baby.

391. Buy generic or store brand baby wash and shampoo. There is little or no difference between the cheaper versions and the more expensive name-brands. Plus, they smell just as good!

392. The dollar store can be a great place to pick up toiletries such as shampoos, lotions, and washcloths for your baby. Sometimes they even carry name brands.

393. Make your own hair detangler by combining one part conditioner with ten parts water. Mix well and pour into a spray pump, using a funnel to avoid spilling.

394. Extend your baby wash by using a suds pump. Fill the pump 1/3 of the way with baby wash, then fill to just an inch below the top with water. A pump cuts down on the amount of liquid soap you have to use, adding air to make a rich foam instead of a concentrated liquid. Pampered Chef makes a great one that sells for less than $10. It is an investment that pays for itself many times over. www.pamperedchef.com

395. Unless you live in a particularly dry climate, you probably won't use very much baby lotion. The lotion the rest of the family uses is fine for baby.

BATH TOYS

396. There's no need to spend money on expensive bath toys for baby. Plastic lids and containers are great for tub time, as well as toys your baby probably already has, like stacking cups, plastic key rings, and teethers. Other great toys include turkey basters, Styrofoam trays, colanders, and sponges.

safety tip

Store all household cleaners in a locked cabinet, safely away from your child.

397. Skip the fancy bath toy holder. Instead, opt for a plain mesh laundry bag (if the bag is too large, simply tie a knot in the bottom). The mesh allows the water to drain, preventing any mold or mildew from forming on your baby's toys. Look for one at your dollar store.

398. A mesh bag that oranges come in also works well for bath toy storage. Hang from the faucet or showerhead to maximize drainage.

399. You can use a large plastic planter to store your baby's tub toys. It has holes in the bottom for drainage, and a tray to collect excess water. Plus, you can use it to plant flowers in when you're done using it for baby.

400. Keep your baby's bath toys clean by throwing them in the washing machine with your shower curtain. Add a little bleach to kill any mildew or bacteria.

FUN STUFF

401. Make your own bath time finger paint by combining shaving cream, food coloring, and a couple tablespoons of non-abrasive, non-toxic cleanser. Your child will have lots of fun "painting" the tub with this concoction!

402. Bath tub soap crayons can be made by mixing 1/2 cup soap flakes (grating a bar of Ivory works well), 1 to 2 tablespoons hot water, and a little food coloring. Place the mixture in molds like ice cube trays or muffin tins until dry (this can take up to a week).

403. Fill your ice cube trays with water, adding a drop of food coloring to each section. When frozen, these can be popped out and placed in baby's bath water. He'll have fun "chasing" them around in the tub and trying to grab for them before they melt.

404. Create your own bubble bath by mixing a little liquid dish soap under the running water. Don't use too much, as the detergent can be harsh on baby's skin.

405. Make your own bath paints. Add a little food coloring to liquid hand soap and place in disposable plastic containers.

CUTTING BABY'S HAIR

406. Cutting baby's hair can be almost as expensive as getting your own hair cut. It's hard to find a stylist that doesn't charge at least $10 for a simple trim. Instead, invest in a pair of hair cutting scissors and learn how to trim your child's hair at home.

407. A vacuum hair cutting system can be used to trim hair of various lengths. It uses the suction power of your vacuum, leaving no mess. They can be found for less than $50 on eBay by searching names like "Flowbee" and "RoboCut."

408. For cutting bangs, place a piece of Scotch tape right at the level you want to cut. Cut just above the line, and the tape comes off with the hair. You'll have less mess and a straighter line.

409. A sun visor can be helpful when cutting your child's bangs. Lay the hair over the visor, and then cut. Your child is less likely to feel anything while you're cutting, and you end up with a straighter line.

Part Four:

Getting Baby Dressed

10

Bargains on Your Baby's Clothes

USED CLOTHING

410. If you're apprehensive about buying used clothing, don't be. Washing it in hot water will get rid of any dirt and germs. Look in your closet. It's ALL used clothing now, whether or not it was purchased that way.

411. Garage sales are a MUST for thrifty parents. This is where you can find used clothing at 75–90 percent off the retail price. Because infants outgrow clothes so quickly, there is very minimal wear and tear. You can get quality name-brand clothes for a steal.

412. Consignment or resale stores are the most expensive places to buy used clothing. Most items are priced about a third or half of what you'd pay for new items. However, they also offer a much wider selection than garage sales or thrift stores. They are great if you're someone who likes designer brands. They are also good when you're looking for something specific, such as a blue shirt to match a certain sweater or a specific type of shoe.

413. Organize a clothing exchange with friends and/or family. Ask participants to save the clothes that their children grow out of or do not want anymore. You can then go through the clothes and see what you want to keep.

414. If you receive hand-me-downs from a friend or relative, be sure to send a thank-you note. It will make the giver feel great about giving you the clothing and make her more likely to want to do it again.

415. When babies begin to crawl, they can be really tough on the knees of their pants. Buy iron-on knee enforcement patches for them. Instead of patching them on the outside, iron them on the inside of the pants. You will get the same benefit and your baby's clothes will look much better.

416. If your baby girl outgrows the length of her pants before the waist, you can cut them off and make them into capris. This works especially well with jeans. Just cut off the pants at the appropriate length, wash to create a fringe, then sew a cute decorative ribbon around the bottom. You can even embellish stains or spots with matching appliqués or bows.

417. If you're concerned about pilling, try to avoid clothing with polyester. One hundred percent cotton clothing is more breathable, comfortable, and causes less skin irritation than synthetic blends.

418. If you decide that you're going to resell your baby's clothing when you're finished using it, it is better to stick to name-brands. The following brands are top sellers among online auction shoppers: Gymboree, Gap, Tommy Hilfiger, Ralph Lauren, and Hanna Andersson. However, don't pay full price for it. Look at discounters like Marshall's, TJ Maxx, and Ross. Even shop garage sales and secondhand stores.

419. When buying sleepwear, make sure it is either flame-resistant or snug fitting. Loose pajamas are more likely to come into contact with a flame and burn more rapidly because of the existence of more circulating air.

420. Never buy clothing with a drawstring. Strings pose a risk of entrapment or entanglement. If you find a great item with a drawstring, just remove it or replace it with elastic.

NEW CLOTHING

421. Most moms have a tendency to over-buy their kids' clothes. They see something cute at a good price and just can't resist. It isn't a bargain if you don't need it! Not only will this help your budget, you'll gain valuable closet space too.

422. Soak new dark-colored clothing in a solution of cold water and 1/2 cup vinegar before washing for the first time. This will set the colors and prevent fading.

423. Leave tags on the clothes you receive as gifts. You may find you don't use them, and leaving the tags on will make returning or exchanging them easier.

424. Don't forget more expensive department stores for high-quality baby clothing. However, walk right past their displays of new merchandise and head for the clearance racks. You can often times find name-brand merchandise for 75 percent off or more.

425. Be sure to wash clothing before the time comes when you think your child will fit into it. Some items will shrink in the wash and be too small for your child to wear.

426. When buying two-piece pajamas, buy more than one of the same style. If one piece becomes damaged or stained, baby can still wear the remaining piece with the other set.

427. When shopping for blanket sleepers, buy the ones without the feet. You will find that they fit your child a lot longer.

428. When buying clothing, consider how easy it will be to get it on your baby. Choose zippers over buttons, and avoid anything that has to be pulled over baby's head. Clothes that are difficult to get on tend to sit in drawers unused.

429. Search eBay for gift cards and merchandise credit slips from your favorite national clothing retailers. Use keywords like "gift card," "credit," "certificate," and "voucher."

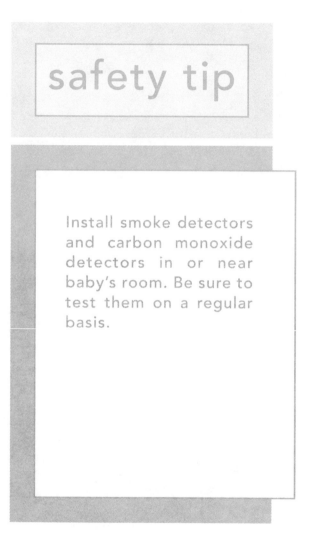

safety tip

Install smoke detectors and carbon monoxide detectors in or near baby's room. Be sure to test them on a regular basis.

430. Shop at the end of the season for your child's wardrobe for next year. You can easily save 75 percent on new clothing. To determine the size to buy, consider what your child's age will be and his growth pattern. Check with parents who have a child a year older to see what sizes their kids are in.

431. Spring merchandise is least expensive in late June. Look for sales to be the best a week or so before the Fourth of July holiday.

432. Summer clothing hits rock-bottom prices in September, with markdowns starting at 50 percent off just after Labor Day. If you wait until the end of September, you can find merchandise for 75 percent off or more.

433. Fall and winter clothing is cheapest in January. Stores will typically mark their merchandise down to 50 percent off right after Christmas. It will go down to 75 percent off or more by the end of January. Shoppers who can wait until February may find even better deals, but selection will be limited.

434. For kids who are especially rough on clothing, consider buying corduroy. Corduroy is more durable than denim and holds up well over time.

435. If sweaters start to show pilling, shave them gently with a disposable razor.

436. If you plan on having more children, try to buy gender-neutral clothing as much as possible. Shop in the boys' section to get clothing that is more durable, and in some cases less expensive. Plus, it is easier to get away with dressing a little girl in blue than it is to dress a boy in anything feminine.

437. *Always* save your receipts. If an item falls apart too soon or shrinks too much the first time you wash it, bring it back to the store with receipt in hand. Most retailers will refund your money on defective merchandise.

438. If you know how to sew, consider making some clothes for your baby. There are many patterns that you can use over again as your baby grows and changes sizes. Or, make your own patterns from existing items in your baby's wardrobe.

SOCKS AND SHOES

439. When buying socks for your baby, buy white socks all in the same brand. Then if you lose one, the remaining sock can be paired with another one. Many moms rave about Old Navy anti-skid socks. The sizes are noted right on the bottom, preventing you from matching two odd-sized socks.

440. Instead of buying socks with the anti-skid sole, which can cost double or triple the price of plain socks, make your own with puffy fabric paint. A little bottle of fabric paint costs about $2 (the price of one pair of anti-skid socks) and will last several seasons. Be creative—write your child's initials on the bottom, the size of the socks, or just cute little designs!

441. Bathtub decals placed on the bottom of your baby's slippers will prevent him from slipping on smooth surfaces, like hardwood floors.

442. Don't buy too many dresses for your 6-to-12-month-old daughter. At this age, she will be crawling or rolling around, and dresses just get in the way. Instead, stock up on sturdy leggings.

443. Don't spend a dime on baby shoes until your child has learned how to walk. Shoes are unnecessary for a child who hasn't learned to walk yet. If you're concerned with keeping your child's feet warm, invest in an inexpensive pair of slippers with elastic around the ankles.

444. Stride Rite shoes have long been considered the standard in high-quality baby shoes. However, a new pair can set you back as much as $50. Stride Rite also manufactures shoes for Target and Sears for much less. The Sears brand is called Munchkins, and the Target brands are Kid Smart and Baby Smart.

445. If the soles of baby's shoes are too slippery, use a little bit of sandpaper to scuff up the bottoms.

446. The Mr. Clean Magic Eraser takes away scuff marks from baby's white shoes. Baby wipes also work well. Correction fluid helps to cover up scuff if it doesn't come off.

447. If your child's shoelaces lose the tip, you don't need to replace them just yet. Try coating the ends with a coat of clear fingernail polish, and you should be able to thread them through the eyelets again.

safety tip

Keep the phone number for the National Poison Control Center in a handy location: 1-800-222-1222.

448. A toothbrush can help clean the threads and lint that get stuck in Velcro shoe closures.

449. KidsNshoes offers an easy-to-use shoe-measuring system. Visit their website to print their measuring system on any standard 8.5 x 11 paper. www.kidsnshoes.com

WINTER GEAR

450. Instead of buying mittens for your baby, use a knee-high sock instead. They keep baby's hands just as warm and aren't as likely to fall off.

451. When considering buying a snow-suit or bunting for your baby, make sure it has legs. While the "bag" styles are nice, you will have a hard time when it comes to getting baby in a car seat.

452. Consider buying an insulated car seat lining with a zippered cover instead of a heavy winter coat. It eliminates one layer of clothing to have to put on your baby. Dress your baby in layers for added warmth.

GETTING THE MOST OUT OF BABY'S CLOTHES

453. Prolong the life of your child's snap-crotch garments by using clothing extenders. Extenders have snaps on both ends that fit most bodysuit brands and add about four inches of length to onesies and rompers for longer wear. They can be ordered from One Step Ahead by visiting their website and searching for "False Bottoms." www.onestepahead.com

454. When your baby is learning to crawl, avoid worn-out knees by making kneepads. You can make them by cutting a few inches off the toe portion of a tube sock and placing it around her knee. Not only do they save your child's clothing from wear and stains, they help protect little knees, too!

455. When packing away your child's outgrown or out-of-season clothing, be sure to store it off the ground to protect it from moisture. Instead of expensive plastic storage containers, use plain garbage bags. Use a vacuum cleaner hose to suck the air out of the bags and tie them securely. Then, place the bags in a cardboard box.

456. If you get a stain on a favorite item of clothing, cover with a cute sew-on appliqué or iron-on transfer, making sure it is attached securely. If the whole thing has been stained, tie-dye it! You can even create coordinating sets (from clothing that previously didn't match) with this technique.

457. New parents receive lots of baby outfits as gifts. Don't feel guilty about returning them or exchanging them for a larger size. Most gift-givers would rather you have something you can use than an item that sits in your closet or is outgrown before it can be used.

458. When your little girl outgrows one of her favorite dresses in length but it still fits on top, pair it with leggings to wear as a top.

459. If your baby son outgrows the length of his pants before the waist, you can cut them off to make shorts.

460. Add a layer of lace to dresses and pants that become too short for your little girl. Make sure you prewash the lace or ribbon before sewing.

461. When your baby outgrows his blanket sleepers with feet in them, cut the feet portion of the sleeper off.

11

Where to Shop and When

BABY CLOTHING RETAILERS

462. TJ Maxx, Marshalls, and Ross are great places to find deals on name-brand children's apparel. They offer the same brands as department stores for 20 to 50 percent off.

463. Join the Sears KidVantage program. Sears will replace clothing that has worn out with the exact same size and brand when you are a member as long as you save your receipt. When KidVantage members accumulate $100 or more in sales, they receive a certificate good for 15 percent off regular and sale merchandise. Membership is free.

464. Target typically marks their kids' clothing down on Mondays (this may vary by store, be sure to check your own store for its markdown schedule). They usually start at 30 percent, then go to 50 and 75 percent if items don't sell. If you're lucky enough to hit their store when a bunch has just been marked down to 75 percent off, stock up. At that discount, their clothes are cheaper than garage sale prices.

465. Like Sears, ShopKo stores also have a wear-out guarantee on their clothing. Their Kid-Tough policy states that if your child rips, tears, or ruins a garment before he outgrows it, ShopKo will replace it in the same size for free.

466. The Children's Place does deep markdowns. Separates like tees, pants, shorts, and shirts can often be found at the end of the season for $2.99 or less.

GAP

467. Wednesdays are a great day to shop Gap because they typically mark down their merchandise in the middle of the week. Ask your local store when they do their markdowns.

468. Gap's final markdowns always end in 7. So if an item is marked $4.99, you know it will go down at least one more time. If it is $3.97, you know that is rock-bottom and you better grab it!

469. If you are a regular Gap shopper, save your receipts. If you stop by their store within two weeks of making a purchase, they will give a price adjustment for clothing that has been marked down within that time. It isn't necessary to bring the clothes, just the receipt.

470. GapCard holders receive an additional 10 percent off their purchases the first Tuesday of each month. For every purchase you make with your Gap card, you earn points towards merchandise vouchers.

471. If you see something on sale at babyGap but not in the right size, have the manager check other stores in your area or on the Web. To avoid the shipping charge, you merely need to order one item at regular price (a pair of socks, for example). Your merchandise is mailed to your door within a few days.

OLD NAVY

472. It is hard to beat Old Navy's clearance racks for cute kids' clothes at reasonable prices. Because they like to turn over their inventory frequently, their clearance racks are often stocked with items for $4.99 and under. They occasionally will have items for $.97 and $1.97. Like Gap, they typically do their markdowns midweek.

473. Sign up for the Old Navy Card and get a $5 merchandise voucher for every $100 you spend, plus other coupons and discounts.

474. Old Navy's price adjustment policy is 7 days. Bring your receipt back to the store within that period of time to receive credit for the difference in price.

GYMBOREE

475. Gymboree's clothing lines are coordinating so buyers can collect pieces to mix and match. For that reason, their clothing is one of the best out there for resale. In-demand items that have been very gently worn occasionally sell on eBay for more than the original retail price!

476. Wait for Gymboree's Circle of Friends Sales (30 percent off) and Gymbucks periods (buy $50, get $25 to spend later) to shop. Combine these sales with clearance merchandise, and you can save quite a bit.

Here's a bonus: Gymboree stores will often only display merchandise from their most recent lines on the sales floor. Clothing from past lines that didn't sell is often stored in the back room. Because these pieces have been around the longest, they've seen the most markdowns. If you ask, you may be able to take a peek or have the sales associate bring out what they have in the size you're looking for.

477. Sign up for the Gymboree Visa card and get an additional 5 percent off your purchases there. Gymboree Visa holders also receive added benefits such as additional discount days, advance notice of sales, and a merchandise voucher when they sign up for the card.

478. Gymboree's price adjustment period is 14 days. If you buy an item of clothing that gets marked down within 14 days of your purchase, bring in your receipt for a credit of the difference. There's no need to bring in the merchandise itself.

safety tip

To prevent strangulation, never leave a bib on your baby while he's playing.

479. When you're at your local Gymboree store, ask the associate if you can sign up for their mailing list. You will get advance notice of special sales.

480. For serious Gymboree addicts, check out the Gymbohaven website. You'll find information on upcoming sales and outlet openings as well as photographs of past and present Gymboree clothing lines.

OUTLET SHOPPING

481. At outlet stores, clothing with cut tags or black marker through the label are taken from the regular stores' inventory. Other clothing may be specially made for the outlet and of a slightly lower quality.

482. Carter's, famous for their durable sleepwear, has outlet stores across the country. Shop the racks in the back for sleepwear at $3 and $5 per set. Some merchandise is irregular, which will be noted on the tag. Visit their website to join their celebration club to receive coupons. www.carters.com

483. The Children's Place website has an online outlet that frequently offers clothing for $3.99 and under. Click on "Shop Outlet" when you visit their site.
www.childrensplace.com

484. Healthtex outlets are found in conjunction with Vanity Fair Outlets across the country.

485. OshKosh outlets are a great source for quality kids' clothing at reasonable prices. Wait to shop their clearance sales, which are held at the end of each season. Clothing can be found at prices 50 to 75 percent off retail. Give the cashier your address and email information to receive coupons for additional savings.

486. Gap Outlet stores carry merchandise from previous seasons along with clothing made exclusively for the outlet. Most moms report that finding bargains at the outlet is hit or miss.

487. Old Navy Outlets carry their own "outlet" line of clothing, which is indicated on their tags. Their prices are less than what you'd find in their regular stores. However, you probably won't be able to do any better than the clearance racks in their regular stores.

488. The Children's Place outlet stores are definitely worth a visit. For the best deals, search the clearance merchandise at the back of the store. Some moms have been lucky enough to find items under a dollar.

489. Gymboree began adding outlet stores in 2004 in New York and Michigan. Their outlets carry first-quality lines from previous seasons at discounted prices. Tags are marked so that returns can only be made to other outlet stores.

490. Visit the Outlet Bound website to search for outlets by store and by location. www.outletbound.com

BUYING ONLINE

491. Check out Yahoo! Groups and search for discussion loops for infants' and children's resale clothing. By joining a discussion group, you receive messages via email from other members related to buying and selling new or gently used children's clothing. Search keywords such as the brands of clothing you prefer, "resale," or "clothing." www.yahoogroups.com

492. Look for online-consignment and thrift stores. Resale.net is a portal that lists many of the resale shops on the Internet. www.resale.net

493. Subscribe to the online newsletters of the clothing stores you like. They will inform you of their sales and often email coupon codes good for free shipping or other discounts.

494. Always check to see if online coupon codes are available to use on your online order. Visit Mommysavers.com for a complete listing of current codes.

TIPS FOR ONLINE AUCTIONS

495. Ask questions. Most items can't be returned, so you'll want to make sure you ask about the condition and size before you place your bid. If anything is vague or omitted, write to the seller and ask before placing your bid.

496. Check the seller's feedback rating. The comments under his feedback profile should be able to tip you off to a disreputable seller.

497. Check shipping costs before placing your bid. Sometimes the high cost of shipping can negate any savings.

498. Look for clothing in lots or groups of more than one item to save money. You can even purchase an entire wardrobe for your child at considerable savings.

499. When buying on eBay, check the seller's other auctions. You may be able to take advantage of combined shipping costs to save money on additional items.

500. Wait as long as possible to place your bid. Otherwise, you will drive up your own price. There are even online services that will place your bid for you in the last seconds of the auction for a small fee.
www.auctionsniper.com or www.powersnipe.com

RESALE SHOPPING AND GARAGE SALES

501. Mondays and Tuesdays are good days to shop thrift stores. Most stores receive more donations on the weekend and put out their new merchandise early in the week.

502. Check to see if your neighborhood thrift stores have "bag sales" or half-off days.

503. Once Upon a Child is one of the leading children's resale shops in the country. Their stores are independently owned and stocked with high-quality used clothing at reasonable prices. To find one near you, visit their website at www.ouac.com.

504. Visit the National Association of Resale & Thrift Shops website to find thrift stores in your area. www.narts.org

505. Garage sales are far and away the most economical way to find kids' clothes at bargain prices. Most kids' clothing is 75 to 90 percent off the original price.

506. Looking for garage sales in wealthier neighborhoods increases your chances of finding high-quality items.

507. On the flip side, don't avoid lower-income neighborhoods if they are advertising items that you need. You may be surprised at the great deals you find.

safety tip

To prevent suffocation, keep all plastic bags out of the reach of your child.

508. Neighborhood garage sales are great because you can go to many sales without having to drive.

509. When the garage sale ads come out, map out your route according to addresses and starting times.

510. If you're really into garage sales, have your neighborhood/hometown map laminated. That way you can mark addresses each week and wipe them off when you're finished.

511. Get to the sale when it starts, or even a little bit early. The good items are always the first to go, so it pays to be one of the first through the door.

512. Bring a few sets of AA, C, and D batteries and a mini screwdriver along in your purse so that you can test electronic toys.

513. If you are lucky enough to hit a sale that has clothing in the exact sizes you need, is of high quality and is priced right, ask the seller to call you before her next sale. She may even let you shop early, allowing you to get the best selection. If you're even more lucky, you can negotiate buying the whole lot of clothing at a reduced price. That saves the seller the time of organizing and pricing her items—you both win!

514. If you're at a good garage sale and are looking for a certain item that you don't see (a snowsuit for example), don't be afraid to ask. Sometimes the seller will have what you want but didn't get around to pulling it out and marking it for the sale.

515. Make sure you check the zippers, buttons, and snaps on clothing you purchase. These items will end up never being worn if they are defective. However, if you don't mind mending, point out the flaw to the seller and ask for a discount.

516. Go a bit later after the big crowds have dissipated. The sellers are usually willing to make a deal on what is left.

517. If you don't like a price, particularly on a big-ticket item, don't be afraid to offer them less than what they're asking.

518. When you find several items you want to purchase, make a single offer for the entire lot. The seller more often than not agrees to the price you offer.

519. If you see something you like at a garage sale, pick it up and carry it with you even if you're not sure you'll buy it. You can always set it down later if you change your mind.

12

Laundry and Cleaning Up

CARING FOR BABY'S CLOTHING

520. Proper care of your baby's clothing will extend its life and help it bring a higher price if you plan on selling it when it has been outgrown. Be sure to pretreat stains and wash special outfits in cold water to minimize fading.

521. When buying laundry detergent, consider the cost per load. Because the amount of detergent needed for a load can vary by brand, the price per ounce isn't a reliable measure of the true cost.

Brands like Purex, Ajax, and All are economical yet do a good job.

522. Make your own laundry soap at home. Combine half a bar of grated Fels-Naptha soap with two pints water. Heat on low until melted. Stir in 1/2 cup Borax and 1/2 cup Washing Soda (found in the laundry aisle) and remove from heat. Pour the mixture into a large bucket and add enough water to make two gallons. Let the mixture stand overnight until it thickens. Use one cup per load.

523. Only put your child's clothing in the dryer for five minutes. That's all the time you'll need to fluff the fabric and get the wrinkles out. Then, hang them to dry.

524. Air-drying not only saves electricity, it extends the life of your clothing. Driers can set in stains and cause fabric to shrink. Hang a clothesline in your basement, invest in a drying rack, or hang clothes on hangers to dry.

525. If your baby has a favorite blanket, cut it in half. That way he'll always have a section to keep when you're laundering the other part. And if you ever lose one half, you'll have a spare.

526. Wash items containing polyester inside-out to reduce pilling and fuzzing.

527. When you're done using your baby gate, lay it flat and use it as a drying rack for sweaters and other clothing.

528. Carry a stain-stick in your diaper bag so you can pretreat a stain when it occurs, making it easier to get out in the wash once you're home.

529. Laundry detergents formulated just for babies are not necessary. Most babies are not bothered by the detergents used by the rest of the family. If your baby does react to stronger detergent, it may be a sign the clothes weren't rinsed well enough. Try running the rinse cycle twice to remove all traces of detergent, or try regular detergents that are fragrance-free.

530. Use a zippered pillowcase as a laundry bag for your baby. Throw the whole thing in the washer and dryer.

531. Use vinegar instead of fabric softener when washing baby clothes. It is much less expensive than commercial fabric softeners and better for your baby's skin. *Make sure you use white vinegar.*

Make sure that any child care provider in your home has the phone number where you can be reached and the phone numbers of baby's doctor and hospital.

STAIN REMOVAL

532. Commercial stain removers most recommended by moms include Totally Toddler spray and Zout.

533. Make your own stain pretreater by mixing one part laundry detergent, one part hydrogen peroxide, and one part water in a spray bottle. Spray stains and rub material together or scrub with a soft brush if needed.

534. To remove formula or other baby stains from baby's white clothing, try the Clorox Bleach Pen. These pens allow you to apply bleach without getting it on the entire piece of clothing.

535. Soak protein-based stains like milk and feces in cold water. Hot water cooks the protein, causing it to coagulate on the fabric's fibers and making it hard to remove.

536. Never put a stained garment in a dryer. The heat from the dryer can set the stain.

537. Fresh formula stains can be removed by using a little meat tenderizer. Mix with water to create a paste, dab on the stain and leave on overnight. The meat tenderizer will eat away the formula stain, which is a protein.

538. Hydrogen peroxide can be used to remove formula stains and yellowing of old garments. Mix a solution of a one part hydrogen peroxide with one part water. Soak the clothes for about half an hour. If the stain is still there, add a little more peroxide and soak for another half hour. Launder as you normally would.

539. Murphy's Oil Soap can also be used for removing formula stains. Apply a small amount to the stain and gently rub with a toothbrush. Wash as you would normally.

540. Baby feces can be removed from clothing by soaking in an enzyme solution such as Biz detergent with a little water. The enzymes eat away at stains.

541. For your toughest stains, make a mixture using 1 cup laundry detergent, 1/2 cup bleach, 1/2 cup dishwasher detergent, and warm water. Soak heavily soiled items overnight, then machine wash. Test garments for colorfastness, as this may bleach some fabrics.

542. Vomit can be removed from clothing by using a mixture of cold water, 1 quart ammonia, and a little detergent.

543. Dawn PowerPlus liquid dish soap is an effective stain remover. It breaks down the tough protein-type stains like feces, baby food, and formula.

CLEANING OTHER ITEMS

544. For items that can't be laundered, clean them with baking soda. Sprinkle baking soda on a damp sponge and use it to clean high chairs, car seats, strollers, and other baby gear.

545. The easiest way to clean a child's plastic toys is to run them through the dishwasher. The high water temperature will also kill germs and bacteria (make sure you never put a toy that requires batteries in the dishwasher).

546. Toys can be cleaned and sanitized using a mild bleach solution (1/4 cup of bleach to 1 gallon of water). Rinse well and air-dry.

547. A garden hose works well to clean off a plastic high chair. Just take your high chair outside, spray with an all-purpose cleaner, and rinse with the hose. Make sure you get in all the nooks and crannies and don't forget the underside of the tray.

548. Crayon can be removed from your walls with WD-40. It can also be used to remove crayon stains from clothing. Just spray on as you would a stain remover and launder as usual.

549. The powerful hoses found at car washes are great for cleaning baby items like strollers, exersaucers, and other baby gear.

550. Clean baby's toys with a mixture of 4 tablespoons baking soda to 1 quart warm water. Disinfectant spray works well on toys that have tiny parts and crevices.

safety tip

Don't use a tablecloth once baby is mobile and can pull it (and whatever is sitting on it) down on himself.

Part Five:

The Newest Room in the House

13

Bedding and Furniture in Baby's Room

BEDDING

551. When purchasing bedding for your first child, choose a gender-neutral color or pattern. Subsequent children will be able to use it regardless of their sex. You can always accessorize in pink and blue.

552. If you're handy with a sewing machine you can easily make your own baby accessories. Bed ruffles, diaper holders, and curtains often come in fabric-panel form at the fabric store, making sewing a breeze. You just have to be able to sew a straight seam.

safety tip

A sock on a doorknob can prevent a child from opening it. Secure it with a rubber band to keep it from coming off.

553. Buy enough fabric to make bedding for a twin-sized bed as well. That way when your baby graduates to a "big" bed, you won't have to completely redecorate his room.

554. If you fall in love with a certain pattern, search for it by keyword on eBay. You may be able to find the exact same thing at substantial savings. eBay doesn't always mean used, either. If you are looking for new bedding, enter keywords such as "NWT" (new with tags) or "NIP" (new in package).

555. Consignment stores, thrift stores, and garage sales often have baby bedding for a fraction of the price of new sets.

556. Pick a pattern with commonly found colors. If you choose bedding in a strange pattern, you'll have trouble finding accessories to match it.

557. If know how to sew, you can use your own worn sheets to make baby sheets, using the less-worn part. They will be nice and soft!

558. Invest in high-quality crib sheets. Look for at least 2 to 3 sheets in 100 percent cotton. They will see more wear and tear than your own sheets, and you'll want ones that will withstand the repeated washings.

559. Keep your receipt when buying crib sheets. If they shrink too much to fit properly, don't use them. If they accidentally come loose, they pose an entanglement risk to your baby.

560. When buying baby's layette, skip the comforter. Babies should not be put to sleep with bulky bedding because it can increase the incidence of sudden infant death syndrome (SIDS). Invest in a nice blanket instead.

561. Don't buy bedding as a part of a set. You will be paying for items you don't really need, like a comforter, a diaper stacker, and a bed ruffle. It is a better bet to buy what you need separately.

562. Whatever pattern you choose, make sure it doesn't have too much white in it. White gets dirtier faster, and it can discolor with a lot of washing.

563. It's not necessary to use a bumper pad for your crib. The ties that secure it to crib bars can pose a safety hazard to your baby. If you do use a bumper pad, trim off excess length after tying to prevent your baby from becoming entangled in the ties.

564. Do not buy your baby a pillow. It puts your baby at risk for SIDS and for suffocation.

565. Overstock.com has a steady supply of crib bedding at up to 75 percent off the retail price. Check back at frequent intervals until you find a pattern you like. Their shipping is reasonable, too.

566. Off-price retailers like TJ Maxx, Marshalls, and Ross are another source for baby bedding and accessories. They often carry designer and name-brand labels at up to 60 percent savings.

567. Target also has great baby bedding at reasonable prices. Be sure to check the endcaps in the baby department for clearance merchandise, which can sometimes be found for 75 percent off. If you find only a few pieces of what you want on clearance, ask their customer service department to call other stores in your area to locate the matching ones.

safety tip

Teach your baby to get off furniture or go down stairs backwards on his tummy.

568. Skip the sleep-positioner. It is designed to keep babies on their back while asleep, reducing the rate of SIDS. If a baby is able to roll from back to tummy his rate of SIDS is greatly reduced anyway, leaving no reason to make him sleep on his back.

FURNITURE

569. Buy used furniture and refinish or paint it so all of the pieces match. Furniture painted with enamel has the added benefit of being easy to clean. Add new knobs or drawer pulls to complete the look.

570. Choose furniture that will easily make the transition to childhood. By selecting pieces that are appropriate for any age, you will save time and money by not having to purchase more later.

571. You don't have to stick to baby stores to find furniture for your infant. Most regular furniture stores and outlets carry a selection of nursery furniture.

572. Check out IKEA for good prices on quality kids' furniture. This Swedish-based retailer has opened many stores in the United States in recent years, and chances are there's one close to you. Because the furniture requires assembly, they are able to offer great prices.

573. A bookcase is a must-have item for your nursery. Your baby accumulates lots of books, and you'll want a place to display them. Invest in one that can be used as your child grows older. Be sure to anchor it to the wall to avoid it accidentally tipping over.

574. Make sure all used furniture you purchase for your baby is splinter-free. Also steer clear of furniture with sharp edges or corners, bolts, or other protruding hardware.

575. Save up to 50 percent buying unfinished furniture and painting or staining it yourself. Be sure to use a non-toxic finish. Look in your Yellow Pages or do a search on the Internet for stores in your area.

576. Instead of a toy box, consider buying a large hamper or wicker basket. You can use it for toys now and other kinds of storage later.

577. Create an occasional table by taking a large plastic garbage can, cutting a wooden plywood circle for the top, and draping with a large tablecloth or coordinating fabric. Use the inside of the garbage can to store blankets, linens, or outgrown clothes.

14

Jazzing Up Walls and Windows in Baby's Room

WALL DECORATIONS

578. Resist the urge to wallpaper your nursery. Paint is one of the least expensive ways to decorate a room, and can be changed easily as your child gets older. If you're set on wallpaper, do a border instead of the entire wall. A border is less expensive and is easier to remove.

579. When painting, use "oops paint"— paint that has been tinted the wrong color. You can usually purchase a can for a few dollars (compared to $15 to $25 a gallon for premium paints) and you can still tint it the color of your choice.

580. Instead of hiring a professional painter/artist to design murals on your nursery walls, try doing it yourself at home. There is an easy way, regardless of whether you possess any artistic talent or not. Find a picture that you want to paint on the wall, take it to your local print shop, and have a transparency made. Rent or borrow an overhead projector and project the image on the wall where you want it placed. Pencil in the design, then paint over it.

581. Consider hiring a college art student to paint a unique design or mural on your nursery walls.

582. If you do decide on a hand-painted mural, opt for a design that isn't too babyish. You will want the option of keeping it intact as your baby grows older.

583. A sky effect is a popular paint treatment for nurseries and can be done either on walls or the ceiling. Apply a coat of flat blue paint as a base. Using a 4-inch decorator's brush, apply white brushstrokes at 45-degree angles. Go over again with white paint with a smaller 2-inch brush to further define cloud shapes. Cover with a wash of six parts water to one part white paint to soften the edges and create a translucent finish.

584. Instead of using wallpaper over your entire wall, consider using Wallies cutouts. Their border cutouts can be arranged in a linear way to look like a border or they can be used individually on craft projects and furniture. Larger cutouts can be used as murals. They are less expensive than wallpaper, and are more easily removed.

585. A cute look for your walls can be created using inexpensive fabric and liquid starch. Purchase fabric with the characters or pattern that matches your décor, and cut out the shapes you want to use. Mix 2 teaspoons starch and 1 cup of water. Soak the fabric in the starch solution, then place anywhere you want on the walls. When you move or get tired of the characters you simply take them off. No mess or stains!

586. Stencil your favorite quotations or ABCs around windows, near the ceiling, or as a border. An Internet search can yield some inspirational quotations or cute sayings.

587. Use bath sponges in baby shapes like ducks or teddy bears to create a border. Dip the sponge in paint, dab off the excess, and apply it to your baby's wall.

588. Shop online to find great deals on the wallpaper and borders you see at expensive stores. American Blinds, Wallpaper & More has great prices and makes it easy to find what you're looking for. Search by book name, pattern or item number, or key word. Save from 25 to 85 percent off most retail store prices. You can find them at www.decoratetoday.com

589. Get older siblings involved in decorating baby's room by using their handprints as a border. Paint the older child's hand and then strategically place his "prints" around the top or mid-section of their room as a border. Or, have friends and relatives do their handprints and sign their names underneath. Paint a horizontal line under the handprints for a more finished look.

590. Many houses and apartments built prior to 1978 contain walls painted with lead-based paint. Lead from paint, paint chips, and dust can cause a range of potentially serious health problems. Take precautions before scraping off lead-based paint or tearing out walls. For more information, visit www.epa.gov or contact the National Lead Information Center at 1-800-424-LEAD.

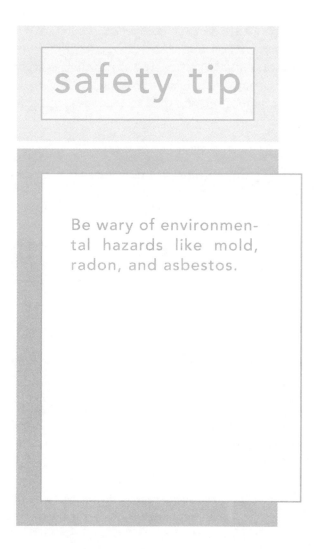

safety tip

Be wary of environmental hazards like mold, radon, and asbestos.

WINDOW TREATMENTS

591. Early in infancy, your baby may have a hard time differentiating between day and night. A room-darkening blind is an inexpensive way to block out sunlight. To finish the look, add a valence that coordinates with baby's room.

592. When window cords are within reach, young children may become entangled and accidentally strangle themselves. The Window Covering Safety Council (WCSC) is dedicated to providing consumer information and educational materials on window-cord safety. They also offer consumers free retrofit devices for repairing cord hazards on older window treatments. Free cord-repair kits can be ordered through www.windowcoverings.org or by calling 1-800-506-4636.

593. Buy an extra sheet or dust ruffle in your pattern of choice, and use it to make coordinating curtains.

594. For a no-sew valance, drape a light-weight fabric around a curtain rod. For a feminine edge, use a fabric like tulle. A fishing net looks cute for boys. You can even do this without a curtain rod, just secure the fabric above your window using a thumbtack.

595. Stain-resistant carpet or hardwood floors are worth the investment. In the first few years of your child's life, he will be spending countless hours on the floor. Make sure you choose a floor covering that can endure the wear and tear.

596. An aquarium can double as a night-light and the bubbling sounds are soothing to baby.

597. Consider installing a dimmer switch in your baby's room. There are certain times you won't want harsh lighting, including feeding times when you get up with your baby in the middle of the night. Adjustable lighting will save you money by avoiding the expense of additional lamps.

598. Consider wall-mounted shelves if you have limited space in your baby's room. This type of shelving is practical not only for babyhood, but for all the things your child will accumulate as she grows older. Ample shelf space leaves enough space on the floor for other items and play space for your baby.

Position your baby's crib away from windows, shelves, or other things that he can either pull down or that could fall on him.

599. Don't install long drapes in your baby's room. Anything long and dangling will be a temptation for your baby to reach up and grab. Shades, blinds, and shorter curtains are safer choices.

600. Make sure windows and screens are secured with stops and locks to safeguard your child against falls. Alternately, open your window to a safe height and pound a small nail into the wood frame above the window, which will keep the window from opening any further.

15

Accessories and Storage in Baby's Room

ACCESSORIES

601. Making your own mobile not only saves money, it allows you to customize it for your baby or to match your decor. Take a set of wooden or cross bars or a metal craft hoop, and hang items from it using fishing line. Use items like laminated photos, small lightweight stuffed animals, or silk flowers. Hang the mobile from a hook on your ceiling using decorative ribbon. Make sure that it is out of your baby's reach and that you remove it once your baby is able to sit up.

602. A shelf can be made for under $20 using a 1 x 6 board and wall brackets. Placed a foot or so below the ceiling, it is great for displaying collectibles, stuffed animals, baby blocks, and other small items.

603. Unfinished wooden pieces like shelves, stools, rocking horses, and other accessories can be found at craft stores for great prices. Finishing and staining or painting them yourself can save a lot of money.

604. Antique or heirloom hats, dresses, and other outfits are an elegant way to dress up a wall. Hang from pegs or hooks.

605. Outgrown infant clothes can be used as a cute wall decoration using twine and wooden clothespins. Secure both ends of the twine against a wall, in the style of an old-fashioned clothesline. Pin articles of clothing on the twine using the clothespins. You can even paint trees on the wall as a mural on which to hang your clothesline.

safety tip

If you have broken glass on the floor, using a broom alone may not pick up all the pieces. Use a wet paper towel to wipe up what's remaining.

606. Avoid using only paint swatches in choosing your paint color. Swatches are often too small to get an accurate feel for what the color will look like in your baby's room. Instead, use larger items like articles of clothing, baby bedding, or other accessories. Bring the actual item to the paint store and they should be able to match it perfectly.

607. Create a display board using a 1 x 6 or 1 x 4 board and clothespins. Paint the board to match your decor, and let dry. Attach the clothespins with nails or a hot glue gun. It's an easy and inexpensive way to create a display of cards, photos, hats, or anything you'd like to display. When your child is older, use it to display his artwork.

608. A decorative ribbon strung across a wall can be used to display cards and photos. Pin them on with clothespins or diaper pins.

609. Use leftover fabric to create a French memo board. Buy a piece of corkboard or foam board and secure the fabric over a piece of batting with a staple gun. Run coordinating ribbons in a diamond pattern over the board.

610. If you have leftover wallpaper, create coordinating accessories using a decoupage medium like Modge-Podge. Cut out characters or pictures from the wallpaper and adhere to lampshades, furniture, stools, or even decorative plates to hang on the wall.

611. Adhere leftover wallpaper to the inside back of a bookcase. It creates visual appeal and helps pull together your theme.

612. Create a custom rug out of carpet remnants. Choose colors that match baby's room and cut the pieces into various shapes patchwork-style and attach them with carpet tape. Attach the entire piece to a rubber rug grip with silicone glue and more carpet tape.

613. Don't forget the ceiling. In the first few months of life, your baby will be spending a lot of time laying on her back. Purchase glow-in-the-dark stars for the ceiling or suspend other interesting objects for your baby to look at.

614. Mosquito netting or tulle draped around the head of baby's crib adds an elegant touch for under $30. Just make sure you remove it by the time the baby is able to pull himself up and grab it.

safety tip

Never let your baby play with small balls, marbles, or balloons. Because they easily block a child's airway, they are associated with more choking accidents than any other toy.

615. An inexpensive kite can add a lot of color to a child's room. Just hang it on the wall or from the ceiling. Add ribbons in coordinating colors on the tail to enhance the look.

616. Use a favorite baby blanket as an organizational accessory in your nursery. Stitch pockets on the front using coordinating fabric. Attach rings to the back and hang it from the wall. The pockets can be used to hold socks, hats, brushes, or other small items.

617. Use the wrapping paper you received baby gifts in to line your baby's dresser drawers.

618. Frame one of your favorite baby cards to make a cute picture. Paint the frame to coordinate with the card and your baby's décor.

619. When buying lamps, shelving, and other accessories, purchase items that your child can use as he or she gets older.

620. While an infant hamper may be cute, it soon is too small to be practical. All those cute outfits fill it up quickly, leaving you wishing you had invested in a larger hamper. Better yet, keep a laundry basket under the crib for this purpose.

621. Make your own bookends using a couple of stuffed animals. Open the seam in the back, remove a little stuffing, and add pebbles or marbles for extra weight. Re-close the seams.

STORAGE AND ORGANIZATION

622. Use baskets for storing toys and toiletries, or use as a laundry hamper. Purchase wicker baskets secondhand and spray paint them white for a clean, new look.

623. If you live in a small house or apartment and are going to be sharing a room with your baby, use a decorative screen to keep baby's space separate from yours.

624. Hang a three-tiered mesh basket from a hook on the ceiling to create more space on dresser tops and changing stations. Use it to store baby wipes or other supplies.

625. A washable area rug is a good investment for baby's room if he's going to use it as a play area. He will be drooling, spitting up, and creating other messes on it.

626. Instead of a mobile, hang soft stuffed toys with fishing line from a hook in the ceiling.

627. If you're short on space, move baby's dresser inside the closet. Because his clothes are so small, there's still space for them to hang above it.

628. To organize infant items, hang a clear shoe organizer on the inside door of your baby's closet. It is great for small items like socks, hats, shoes, and booties, and you can see them all at a glance. Store little toys and other small items that would otherwise get lost in the closet in the remaining pockets.

629. A net hung in the corner near the ceiling can be a great place to store stuffed animals.

Part Six:

The Wide World of Baby Gear

16

Buying Baby Gear

GEAR UP OR GEAR DOWN?

630. Don't buy any piece of baby gear unless you know you're going to use it. It is easy to get carried away buying things for baby, only to have them take up space in your home and gather dust. If you're considering buying large items like swings, bouncers, and exersaucers, give them a test-run while visiting friends to see which items your baby really likes.

631. Consider buying items like exersaucers, bouncy seats, or activity gyms at garage sales or thrift stores. These items will be used for a short period of time before they're outgrown, so you won't want to invest too much money.

632. Borrow baby gear from a friend or family member if she is done using it for one child but doesn't have another child to use it yet. She will most likely be thankful to free up the space for additional storage, and be glad to have someone else put it to good use.

633. Get baby gear for free by joining a Freecycle Network. Freecycle is an online electronic forum that allows its members to give and get items for free in their own local area. Each group is run by a local volunteer moderator and membership is free. www.freecycle.org

634. While finding bargains for your baby can be hit or miss, Big Lots warehouse store can be a great source for inexpensive gear like exersaucers, toys, and even furniture. They currently have over 1400 stores in 46 states. To find a store in your area, visit their website. www.biglots.com

635. Don't be afraid to negotiate with salespeople on high-ticket items. You increase your bargaining power if you are able to buy multiple items from the same store. You may even be able to get a group of parents together (from a childbirth class, for example) to buy together and get a bulk-rate discount.

636. Avoid licensed products. Car seats, strollers, and other baby gear with designer names and characters cost up to 30 percent more than the same thing without them.

637. Don't get too emotional when shopping. It is easy to fall in love with all the cute baby things you see at the store. Go with a clear plan and shopping list and try not to stray from it.

638. Don't trust salespeople to steer you in the right direction. While most salespeople are fairly honest, they are trained to sell you as much as they can.

639. Ask for advice from other parents. Ask your friends what they liked and didn't like about their stroller, high chair, or other baby gear.

640. Check out buying guides from the library. *Consumer Reports* publishes a buying guide to baby gear and also publishes new reports on diapers, strollers, and other baby items in their magazine.

641. Read product reviews on the Internet. Babies "R" Us through Amazon.com has product reviews right on their site. Sites like ePinions.com also offer buying advice on baby gear. Discussion boards are also great places to conduct your own informal surveys of what parents like and don't like.

642. Don't invest in any big-ticket item until you've done a fair amount of comparison shopping. Be sure to demonstrate the product and its features as thoroughly as you can. If it folds up, try folding it. Try all the latches, buckles, and other features. As you try them out, you'll begin to develop your own opinions about what is important to you as the end-user. Bring along a notebook to take notes on prices and other features you find important.

643. If you know you are going to use something a great deal, such as a stroller or backpack, do some research and get the best you can find. Yard sale or consignment shop finds are great, but don't skimp or you will end up wasting your money on two or three of them!

safety tip

Make sure outdoor play areas have sand or another loose material underneath to cushion falls.

644. Check to see how easily you can repair or obtain replacement parts for big-ticket items before making your purchase. Certain brands that are well built may cost more initially, but if they are easily serviced, they can end up costing you less than cheaper brands. Parts and repairs cost only a fraction of the cost of replacement.

645. Save your receipts and packaging. If anything goes wrong with a major purchase, don't hesitate in taking it back to the store. Without a receipt you don't have much recourse.

646. Pay for major purchases with a credit card. Most major retailers can now look up your transaction without a receipt by scanning the item and your credit card.

647. Send in the product registration card. If your purchase is recalled, you'll be contacted by the manufacturer for a replacement or repair kit.

648. Avoid using layaway if at all possible. While it may seem like a good idea to pay for big purchases on an installment plan, you run the risk of having the item sell out before you pick it up. When that happens, you may be forced to accept a floor model or forfeit your down payment.

649. If you do have an item that has been recalled, you may still have some recourse. The manufacturer can send you repair kit or even a coupon/voucher to put towards a replacement if you have an item that has been recalled.

650. When you do buy new items, save the instructions, box, and packaging. When it comes time for resale, your item becomes much more marketable.

651. Look for items that will serve your baby into childhood. High chairs that convert to boosters, baby furniture that can be used into childhood, and other transitional pieces are all wise investments. The longer your child is able to use a particular item, the bigger bang you'll get for your buck.

SHOPPING ONLINE

652. Figure in shipping costs when making your purchase. What may seem like a bargain online may not be one at all after costly shipping charges are factored in.

653. Many sites don't charge you for sales tax. This can be a huge savings on a big-ticket purchase, even negating big shipping charges. Make sure you find out before making your purchase.

654. Check several websites to compare costs. If you see an item that doesn't vary by more than a dollar or two either way, consider buying it in the store. The manufacturer most likely has listed a pre-set cost, and by buying it in the store you'll save shipping costs.

655. Babies "R" Us has an online outlet store. You can sometimes find great deals on baby gear like bouncers, strollers, cribs, and more. Go to www.babiesrus.com and click on the "Baby Outlet" tab.

656. Strollers 4 Less isn't only a great source for strollers, they stock plenty of other baby gear too. Click on their "Store Specials" tab. www.strollers4less.com

657. eBay has every type of baby gear imaginable. There are some great deals to be found on both new and used items. However, make sure you figure in shipping costs before placing your bid. The size and weight of certain items make shipping costs outweigh the benefits of using eBay.

658. Overstock.com has baby bedding, furniture, strollers, and other baby items in stock on a regular basis. They offer low shipping prices as well, making some of the deals you find on their site especially good finds.

659. Look for online codes to use with your purchase. For a listing of online coupon codes, visit www.Mommysavers.com.

660. Check price comparison sites like Shopping.com. Shopping-bots search different sites for prices and the site displays the prices together on one page for quick comparison.

SAFETY GEAR AND ACCESSORIES

661. If you have cabinets that standard safety latches won't fit, or you just don't want to drill holes in your cabinetry, try self-adhesive, industrial-strength Velcro instead.

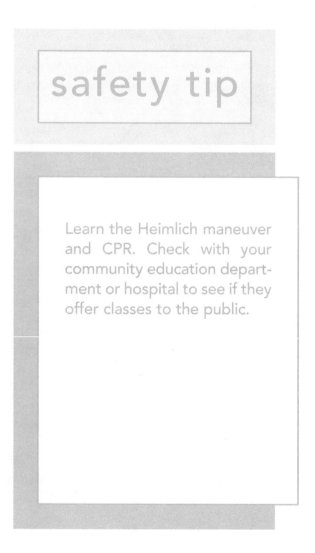

safety tip

Learn the Heimlich maneuver
and CPR. Check with your
community education department or hospital to see if they
offer classes to the public.

662. Instead of purchasing a "choke tube" (a device that tests toys to see if they pose a choking hazard), use an empty roll of toilet paper. It is about the same size as a choke tube and completely free. If an item fits inside the tube, it is small enough to pose a choking hazard to baby. It's great to give to older siblings to test their own toys.

663. Slide a yardstick or dowel through drawer handles to help prevent your baby from opening them.

664. For a baby learning to crawl, there are so many little things on the floor that are tempting to pick up and put in his mouth. Cover your baby's hands with socks so that he can't pick anything up while crawling around.

665. Drape a towel or blanket over the top of a door so that baby won't be able to slam his fingers in it. A sock on a doorknob can prevent a child from opening the door.

666. Shop for safety latches, outlet covers, and other safety devices at home improvement stores or dollar stores rather than at baby stores. You can find the same thing for much less.

667. Buy a safety gate from a home improvement or pet store. Chances are you'll spend less at one of these stores than at a baby superstore.

668. Don't use the older baby gates with the accordion-style bars with V-shaped openings. They pose an entrapment and strangulation hazard.

669. Install a hook-and-eye latch at the top of a door you don't want your child to open. Alternately, attach a bell so that you can hear when the door has been opened.

670. Put inexpensive stickers or decals on sliding glass doors so baby doesn't walk into them.

671. Pad table corners with foam pipe insulation tubes you can get at any home improvement store. Just slit the tube lengthwise and you have an inexpensive, yet effective, way to protect baby from sharp edges. Better yet, remove the table completely until baby is steadier on his feet.

PLAY YARDS

672. If you don't travel often, you may not need a play yard. They are more often used as portable cribs than playpens. Cribs can often be rented in hotels for a minimal charge and may be less expensive than buying a play yard.

673. Don't splurge for the bassinet option on a play yard unless you'll be using it as your primary bassinet. These inserts make it easy on your back when baby is small. However, you may find it's not worth spending the extra $30 for the few times you may use it.

674. If the mesh in your play yard becomes torn, use dental floss to mend it. Dental floss is strong, durable, and will often match the mesh of your play yard.

675. A hard plastic pool serves as an outdoor playpen for crawlers.

BABY MONITORS

676. Consider whether or not a baby monitor is really necessary for your home. Most parents sleeping even several rooms away from their baby are awakened easily when baby cries. If your baby will be sleeping on another level or you will be spending time outside while baby naps, then a monitor will be worth the investment.

677. If you buy a new baby monitor, be sure to save the packaging and the receipt. Some monitors pick up cell and cordless phone signals from neighbors nearby, making it hard to hear your baby's cries. Have the necessary items for a return in case you need to exchange it.

BABY BLANKETS

678. This is something parents rarely have to spend money on, due to its popularity as a baby gift. Don't spend a dime on one until *after* your baby has arrived and you've received the majority of the gifts you expect you'll receive.

679. Make your own no-sew baby blanket with polar fleece. Since fleece won't fray or ravel, you can simply cut the ends without finishing any seams. Or, create a decorative finish with a blanket stitch or fringe edge. For the blanket stitch, use a coordinating yarn color and loop from one side to the other about a half inch from the edge, hooking the last stitch as you go so there is a line that runs along the top. A fringe edge can be made by cutting lines 3 inches long about 1/2 inch apart. You can even do a two-tone blanket by layering two different fleeces together and tie fringe from each side together.

DIAPER BAGS

680. Don't buy a diaper bag before your hospital stay. Formula manufacturers usually give them to hospitals and stock them with samples to give to new parents. If yours doesn't, be sure to ask.

681. The free diaper bags that hospitals give away are the smaller models, and you may find yourself needing a bigger bag for overnights or longer trips. You may be able to make do with a backpack, duffle bag, or small suitcase you already have for such occasions. Don't buy a bigger bag unless you're sure you're going to use it.

682. Buy a pattern dad will feel comfortable carrying, too. If the diaper bag you select is too feminine, he may be reluctant to tote it around. Lands' End and Eddie Bauer both make masculine-looking bags that can be used later as luggage.

683. Patterns for homemade diaper bags can be found at fabric and craft stores. Making your own may not be as difficult as you may think and allows you to customize the fabric pattern.

684. Consider buying a soft insulated cooler to use as a diaper bag. Choose a large-sized bag or backpack style with ample room for diapers, wipes, and feeding gear. It will keep your bottles the right temperature, and can be used long after your baby is out of diapers.

685. Visit Enfamil's website for a coupon for a free diaper bag. Just click on the "Hospital Gift" link, print out the coupon and bring it along to the hospital. www.enfamil.com

17

Getting Around

CAR SEATS

686. Experts recommend buying a new car seat unless you know its exact history. Car seats that have been in accidents may have damage to the frame that you can't see or check for. Such damage could compromise your own baby's safety if you were to have an accident.

687. Make sure the upholstery on your car seat can be removed and washed.

688. Check to see if your county has a program for buying car seats at a reduced rate. Your hospital should be able to provide you with information on whether or not such a program exists in your area.

689. Your insurance company may offer a program to buy car seats at a reduced rate. It is worth investigating.

690. You can save a little money if you buy one convertible seat to accommodate your baby from birth to 40 pounds. However, you'll soon find that an infant-only seat may be easier for you to use and may fit your newborn baby better. An infant-only seat can be carried with you wherever you go without waking a sleeping baby.

691. When shopping for a car seat, ask the salesperson if you can test it in your car before buying. Some fit better than others. If this isn't possible, be sure to save your receipt to make a possible return easier.

692. Look online before shopping for a car seat. This organization has an online database allowing you to see which car seats are most compatible with your make and model of vehicle. www.carseatdata.org

693. Search the Consumer Product Safety Commission (CPSC) database for recent recalls and news releases regarding baby items. Search by category, brand, or date of recall. www.cpsc.gov

694. The National SAFE KIDS Campaign is a nonprofit organization dedicated to the prevention of unintentional childhood injury. Their website includes links to child seat inspection stations, product recommendations, and current information on policies and recalls. Visit them online at www.safekids.org

695. Carseat.org is a good online resource for parents to investigate before purchasing a car seat. Its website includes information on recalls, laws, and regulations regarding car seats. www.carseat.org

696. Skip the mirrors that allow you to look at your baby in a rear-facing car seat. They can be dangerously distracting for drivers.

697. If you do invest in a sunshade for baby, look for a big one. Too often standard sizes don't provide enough shade for baby, making them completely useless.

safety tip

Don't ever ride with your baby on your lap or put an infant in a car seat in the front of a vehicle with air bags.

698. Sometimes salespeople will try and sell you an extra base to put in your second vehicle. It isn't necessary. Infant car seats can be used without the base, by threading the vehicle's safety belt through slots in the infant seat itself (check your own seat for instructions). Safety experts have found that the base provides no added protection, and the seat is just as safe to use without it.

699. Skip the head positioner for car seats if yours doesn't come with one. This stage doesn't last long, a month or two at the most. Instead, roll up a hand towel and place around baby's head to keep it steady.

700. Don't buy a seat protector or mat to go under your baby's car seat. While they are designed to save the upholstery of your vehicle from any damage, they can compromise the fit of the car seat itself.

STROLLERS

701. Only buy a double stroller if you are having twins or will have kids within two years of each other. Not only is it a big expense, it can be hard to maneuver and heavy to take in and out of your car.

702. Instead of buying an inexpensive double stroller which can run over $100, buy two umbrella strollers and use stroller connections. The umbrella strollers are usually under $20 each and connections can be purchased for about $12. When not in use, the connectors can be easily removed so that the strollers can be used separately.

703. Baby Trend makes a double stroller that parents with older children often prefer to traditional models. Their Sit-N-Stand models have a bench seat and also a platform, allowing older kids to stand or sit. It also accommodates an infant car seat in the front seat as well.

704. Don't invest your money in frames that are designed to carry a car seat. Travel systems cost just a bit more, and you have a complete stroller to use when your baby is too big to fit in his infant seat.

705. Before buying a travel system or other large stroller, be sure you test it in the trunk of your car. Too many parents have purchased and assembled them only to find out they don't fit.

706. Consider a carrier instead. A front- or backpack carrier works well and leaves your arms free to do other things than push a stroller.

707. When you're shopping for a stroller, consider how much you'll be using it. If you're an urban dweller who will be using it on a daily basis, opt for the highest quality stroller your budget allows. If you're only going to be using it for occasional trips for the mall, a nice lightweight or umbrella stroller may be all you need.

708. When shopping for an umbrella stroller, make sure it has a basket underneath and a sun shade. These features cost a little bit more, but are worth the price.

709. Never hang purses or diaper bags from stroller handles. The extra weight could cause the stroller to tip over. Use the basket underneath the stroller to store extra items.

710. Search for last year's model. Stores will often offer last year's models at greatly reduced rates to make room for new models. The best time to look for deals is November through January. Oftentimes, the only difference is the fabric pattern. If you can't find one in a store, do a search on the Internet using last year's model.

711. If mosquitoes are a problem in your area, you will probably consider buying an insect net for your stroller. However, a little bug repellent on your baby's clothing will accomplish the same thing. Be sure to use one that is deet-free.

712. Instead of buying a stroller bar with toys attached, attach some of baby's own toys using rings.

CARRIERS AND SLINGS

713. A front-pack carrier or sling is also great to have. Unlike strollers, they free up your hands and are extremely portable. Look for a model with sturdy construction and enough support for baby's head and body. Look for a gently used carrier at consignment stores, garage sales, and even on eBay.

safety tip

Remove insect repellents, mousetraps, or other hazards that may be on the floor unmonitored.

714. If you love the outdoors, you may want to consider a baby back pack. These are great from about age 6–18 months. If you can't find a used one at a thrift store, garage sale, or resale shop, check a used sporting goods store such as Play It Again Sports. The same goes for a baby bike trailer.

715. If you know how to sew, consider making your own baby sling. A pattern for making one can be purchased online from Elizabeth Lee Designs.
www.elizabethlee.com

BOUNCERS, SWINGS, JUMPERS, AND WALKERS

716. Most parents will tell you a bouncer or a swing is a must-have. Swings and bouncers pretty much do the same thing: soothe a fussy baby with a swinging or vibrating motion. Buy one or the other, but not both.

717. If your baby uses a swing or a vibrating bouncer on a frequent basis, invest in rechargeable batteries. You will use them later for toys or other electronic gadgets.

718. If you do buy a swing, consider an open-top model that allows you to put baby in and take him out easily without bumping his head. Also, consider whether or not you'll want to transport your swing. If you do, purchase one of the new compact, portable designs that allow you to fold the swing and take it with you. These features are often worth the additional expense.

719. A stationary exerciser is a great item to have. However, try not to buy a new one. Used models are frequently seen at secondhand stores and garage sales. Because of their size they are cumbersome to store, and parents typically want to unload them as soon as their baby no longer uses it.

720. Don't buy a walker. There have been more accidents with this particular piece of baby gear than any other, most of which occur when baby is sent tumbling down a flight of stairs. They can also be dangerous because they put baby at a higher level to reach things or pull things down on himself. Accidents aside, walkers easily scratch hardwood flooring, scrape walls, and don't always work well on carpeting. You're better off keeping your baby in a stationary exerciser.

721. A jumper is another item to steer clear of. They have been associated with a lot of accidents when their springs have broken or come undone. Not all jumper models will fit your particular door or molding. Instead, buy a stationary exerciser that allows your baby to simulate a jumping motion.

18

Baby Furniture

ROCKING CHAIRS AND GLIDERS

722. Many people would have you believe a glider rocker is an indispensable item. While they are nice for feedings, a traditional rocking chair, recliner, or a comfortable couch will do just as well.

723. If you buy a glider, make sure it is one you can incorporate into your décor after you've moved on from nursing or bottle-feeding. A lot of people don't think the traditional models are aesthetically pleasing and shop around for hipper or more sophisticated looks. Buy a neutral upholstery pattern, skipping the one that only matches your nursery.

724. Skip the expensive coordinating ottoman if you do buy a glider. A sturdy stool will work just as well and cost a fraction of the price.

725. If you purchase a rocker, make sure it has arms. It is easy for new parents to overlook this feature, but you will need something to rest your own arm on when nursing or breast-feeding your baby.

BASSINETS AND CRADLES

726. Bypass a crib altogether and bring your baby into bed with you, a practice known as co-sleeping. While it does save money, it's not without controversy. The American Academy of Pediatrics doesn't recommend co-sleeping due to concerns about the risk of suffocation. On the other hand, psychologists believe that sleeping in a family bed strengthens a baby's sense of security. Check with your pediatrician before trying this method.

727. Arm's Reach Products makes a co-sleeping bed the same height as an adult bed that securely links with yours. It costs less than a traditional crib and also converts to a play yard.

728. If you're going to be using a bassinet, consider buying a play yard with a built-in bassinet feature. It is less costly than a new bassinet, and you'll be able to use the play yard for other purposes.

729. Bassinets are handy to keep in your room because you don't have to walk a long way to get baby for nighttime feedings. Since they are typically only used a few months, look for a secondhand model. Garage sales, thrift stores, and secondhand boutiques are a great source. Again, make sure it meets current safety standards and has never been recalled.

730. If you're using a bassinet, there's no need to purchase special sheets or bedding. A standard size pillowcase should fit right over the little mattress. Plus, you'll get to use it long after your baby has outgrown the bassinet.

731. An old-fashioned style carriage with a bassinet feature can be used as a regular bassinet. It has the added advantage of being on wheels so you can move baby around your home as needed. Plus, the bassinet feature can be removed so the carriage can be used as a regular stroller later.

732. When buying a bassinet that has legs that fold for storage, make sure the locks function well to avoid a potential collapse while it is in use.

733. Don't spend your money on a cradle. They cost more than bassinets and are harder to move around. Either purchase a bassinet if you're looking for a newborn bed, or go right to a crib.

CRIBS

734. An inexpensive crib is just as safe as an expensive model. Because of strict government guidelines, all cribs made in North America must adhere to the same safety regulations. This means that the crib bought at the discount store is just as safe as the one purchased in an upscale baby boutique.

735. Experts advise against purchasing a secondhand crib because a used model may not meet current safety standards. Important pieces of hardware may get lost or get bent, or screw holes may wear out. The glue that holds cribs together can deteriorate when they've been stored in super-hot attics or damp basements.

736. Don't use a crib that has broken or missing parts, even if it appears safe.

737. For complete crib safety information and news on recalls, visit the Danny Foundation's website. The Danny Foundation was founded in 1986 to educate parents about crib safety and to help prevent unnecessary deaths and injuries associated with crib use.
www.dannyfoundation.org

738. When selecting a crib, be sure that you test the crib rail release. Some are easier to manage than others. If you find yourself stuck with one that is sticky, you're in for a long period of frustration!

739. Look online. Overstock.com occasionally stocks name-brand cribs for up to 50 percent off their retail price. Best of all, their shipping prices are incredibly reasonable. Selection is limited, so start shopping early.

740. Don't buy an odd-shaped or non-standard-sized crib, such as those manufactured overseas. You will find it difficult to find bedding that fits.

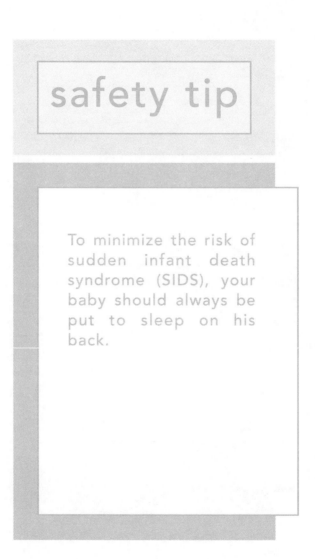

safety tip

To minimize the risk of sudden infant death syndrome (SIDS), your baby should always be put to sleep on his back.

741. While there are many secondhand baby bargains to be found on eBay, it's likely a crib is not one of them. Because you're unable to inspect the crib yourself before buying, stick to looking for new ones.

742. You may be able to purchase a new crib on eBay. However, be cautious. Shipping costs may negate any savings you get, and be sure that you are dealing with a reputable seller. Carefully read all feedback comments and make sure he has a long track record of satisfied customers.

743. Let your fingers do the walking. If you find yourself falling in love with a particular crib model, do your homework. Find out the manufacturer and model number. Look up the manufacturer on the Internet, then call and ask if there are other retailers in your area selling the same thing for less.

744. Cribs with two sliding rails are more expensive than those with one. You really just need one side that slides, since you will likely face one side toward the wall.

745. Don't forget to flip baby's crib mattress as you would your own. This will prevent it from getting too much wear in one spot.

746. Discounters like Target and Wal-Mart offer cribs at a substantial savings. And since all cribs manufactured in the United States and Canada must meet current safety standards, you're not compromising safety by purchasing an inexpensive model.

747. JCPenney is a source for quality cribs that run a little bit less than furniture stores. You may be able to order it on sale and have it shipped directly to your home. However, be wary of shipping costs. Most of the time you can save quite a bit by having it shipped to the store and picking it up there.

748. Baby superstores such as Babies "R" Us sometimes offer sales on certain crib models as loss leaders to bring parents into their store. Start watching their sale fliers until you find a model you like that has been significantly reduced.

749. Crib slats should be no more than 2-⅜" apart (you shouldn't be able to fit a can of soda in between the slats). Make sure none are broken, loose, or splintered.

750. Tighten all screws on your crib and make sure all other hardware is intact.

safety tip

Never leave your baby in a crib with the side rail lowered.

751. Your crib mattress should fit snugly within the crib frame. You shouldn't be able to fit more than two fingers between the mattress and the side of the crib.

752. Avoid a crib with corner post extensions. The corner posts should be no more than 1/16" higher than the end panels.

753. The crib should have no decorative cutouts on the headboard or footboard. Baby's head could get trapped in them.

754. Your baby doesn't need an expensive mattress. A simple yet firm foam mattress will give baby the support he needs. Because it is lightweight, it will make changing sheets easier.

755. A mattress pad isn't necessary for your crib. Crib mattresses are waterproof, so there is no need for additional protection from leaky diapers and spit-ups.

756. A crib that converts to a toddler bed may sound like a great idea, but not if you expect to have another baby while your older child is using the converted bed. Also, most convertible cribs require special mattresses, rails, box spring, mattress extenders, and other assembly hardware that cut into the amount of money you are saving.

757. When buying a crib, make sure the mattress level is adjustable. As soon as your baby is able to sit up, lower his crib mattress to prevent him from falling over the sides.

758. When your baby is too big for his crib, go right to a regular twin-sized bed and skip the toddler bed altogether. Instead, use safety rails or put the mattress directly on the floor if you're worried he may fall out during the night. In doing so, you'll save the expense of a toddler bed and have one less transition to go through with your child.

759. When baby outgrows his crib, you can use the mattress as a stow-away bed for children who come to visit. The mattress is easily stored out of sight by sliding it under a regular twin-sized bed.

HIGH CHAIRS

760. Make sure your high chair not only has a safety belt, but that it also has a third strap that goes between baby's legs. Avoid high chairs that have the strap attached to the feeding tray. When the tray is removed, your child isn't protected.

761. You don't need a high chair with all the bells and whistles. Skip the ones with toys attached, which make it harder to clean. Don't buy one with wheels either. Older siblings *love* to push them around, which could cause an accident. Adjustable heights aren't necessary, either. Buy the model with the fewest features that still meets your needs.

762. A reclining high chair isn't a necessary feature, and can even be dangerous. Babies that aren't old enough to be sitting up on their own shouldn't be in a high chair. Feeding a child in a reclined position puts him at a higher risk for choking.

763. Pay attention to the tray. Make sure it wraps around the baby on the sides; otherwise, you'll have extra cleaning up to do. Test it to see how easily it can be removed. Models that can be removed with one hand are particularly nice.

764. Make sure you buy a high chair that is easy to clean. Avoid cloth upholstery at all costs. Vinyl padding cleans up much more easily.

765. Babies tend to slide around in wooden high chair seats, even when they're buckled in properly. Create a non-skid surface for your baby's high chair by cutting rubber shelving paper to fit the seat.

766. A shower curtain liner cut in squares makes a great spill mat to place under your child's high chair. Look for inexpensive liners at your dollar store.

767. The First Years makes a booster seat that straps onto a dining room chair to be used in place of a high chair. It has a removable tray just like a high chair, and it can be used without the tray as a regular booster seat when your child is older. It comes apart for easy transport and can even go in the dishwasher.

CHANGING TABLES

768. It isn't necessary to purchase a changing table. Once your baby is out of diapers, this piece of furniture becomes useless. Most moms will say it is just as easy to change their baby on the floor, on a bed, or in the crib.

769. If you decide you do want a changing table, invest your money in furniture that will stand the transition from baby to childhood. Consider putting your money towards a nice dresser that can accommodate a changing pad on top.

770. Be sure that changing tables come complete with safety straps. Even if your baby is strapped onto the changing table, always keep one hand on him at all times.

771. Your changing table can be used as a laundry station when you're done with it. Move it to your laundry room and use the compartments to store laundry supplies. The top portion can be used for folding and stacking clothes.

772. King-sized pillowcases work well as changing pad covers. When purchased on clearance, they are affordable enough to have plenty on hand.

Part Seven:

Keeping Baby Busy

19

Toys

EXPENSIVE TOYS AREN'T BETTER TOYS

773. Buy toys at rummage sales or thrift stores. Your baby won't realize that items aren't brand new. If you're squeamish about germs, disinfect them with a little bleach and water before giving them to your child.

774. Hand-me-down stuffed animals may be infested with mold spores and other allergens. Put them in a tied-off or zippered pillowcase and throw them in the washer on hot to kill any bacteria. If they can't be machine-washed, sprinkle them with a little baking soda or cornstarch and let sit for 15 minutes. Dust or shake off the excess.

775. When purchasing secondhand toys, make sure you don't have an item that may be dangerous for your child. Visit www.recalls.gov for a free and complete listing of toys that have been recalled.

776. Make large plastic toys (such as Little Tikes) purchased secondhand look like new with a coat of Krylon Fusion spray paint. This top-selling paint is the first of its kind that bonds directly to most plastics.

777. Instead of buying new toys, exchange a box of your toys with a box of your friend's or neighbor's toys. If you have a lot of toys, put them into storage and rotate them each week.

778. Borrow toys from a lending library. To search for one in your area, visit the USA Toy Library Association's website. Just enter your city and state, and you'll receive a complete listing of the lending libraries in your area. http://usatla.deltacollege.org

779. The best time of the year to buy toys is January, when retailers are clearing out their unsold Christmas inventory. It isn't unusual to find popular toys at 50 or even 75 percent off. Try to anticipate which toys you will want your child to have for birthdays and even next Christmas and stock up.

780. Toys "R" Us through Amazon.com runs some great sales throughout the year. January and July seem to be the best months to shop. Look for the "Free Shipping" symbol on certain toys to avoid shipping charges. Parents can read product reviews before purchasing and avoid paying sales tax.

781. Do not allow babies to play with toys that have missing parts. If you lose a piece to a toy, call the manufacturer. Most will replace the item for free or at cost.

782. An expensive toy box isn't necessary. Wicker baskets, plastic crates, laundry baskets, and Rubbermaid containers all work just as well and can be used for other things after you're done using them to store toys. A plastic garbage can works well to store outdoor playthings.

783. A drawer makes a great toy box, especially in rooms where you need to get work done while baby plays (such as the kitchen, bathroom, or laundry room).

784. Toy chests are often an unrecognized hazard. Make sure yours has safety hinges installed to prevent the lid from slamming shut on baby's fingers or head. It should also have ventilation holes to prevent suffocation in case your child should get trapped inside.

785. Storage containers that have plastic drawers work well to store toys. Label each drawer by category, such as rattles, plush toys, or books.

786. Save your ice cream buckets. They work well to store small toys, crayons, and other small playthings.

787. Juvenile Products Manufacturers Association has information about the safe use of juvenile products, new and innovative products, and related links. www.jpma.org

788. Use plastic shower curtain rings instead of more expensive connecting rings for your baby's toys. You can usually find them at the dollar store. They link together and can be used to hang toys from your stroller or can even be suspended from the ceiling above where you change the baby.

789. Discovery Toys has great toys for babies and young children. Host a party and earn credit towards free products. To find a consultant near you, visit their website at www.discoverytoysinc.com.

790. The Consumer Product Safety Commission (CPSC) has the authority to recall dangerous toys and products from the market. If you think a toy or product is hazardous, contact the CPSC and submit a report by calling 1-800-638-2772 or visiting their website at www.cpsc.gov

791. Avoid choking hazards. Do not buy small toys or toys with small parts for young children.

safety tip

Remove the knobs on
your stove when not in
use and use back burners
whenever possible.

792. Plastic measuring cups and spoons are great to use as nesting toys.

793. Use a clear plastic 20-ounce soda bottle to create an interesting toy for baby. Place objects inside such as aluminum foil balls, pieces of sponge, fabric swatches, glitter, or sequins. Fill with a little water and superglue the cap on tightly.

794. Make a sock puppet using Dad's worn out gym socks. Make sure you embroider the eyes, nose, and mouth instead of using buttons or other objects that could be choking hazards.

795. Make your own rattle using a clear plastic soda bottle or another small container. Insert objects like beans, unpopped popcorn or pasta, pebbles or rice. Secure the lid tightly with a little superglue.

796. Make a beanbag with scraps of material and dried beans or unpopped popcorn. Stitch securely.

797. Babies love crunching sounds. Take an old tube sock and insert some crinkly cellophane, tin foil, or wrapping paper. Tie off the end and you have a fun toy.

798. Create a "color book" for your baby by taking pictures of items around your home in certain colors (for example, red ball, green plant, or blue brush). Better yet, have baby wear the specific color and pose her in the picture as well. Put the photos in a small 4 x 6 photo album that you can find at a dollar store.

799. Make your own shape sorters. Use cookie cutters to trace two or three different shapes on a coffee can or ice cream bucket lid (cut the holes slightly larger than the trace line). Use the same cookie cutters to cut shapes out of heavy-duty cardboard for baby to insert through the holes.

800. Make your own simple puzzles for baby by gluing snapshots or pictures from magazines onto a piece of sturdy cardboard. When the glue is dry, cut into desired shapes. If the cardboard is rough, use an emery board to sand the edges.

801. Take several ladies' silk scarves and tie them together end to end, the way a magician would. Insert them into a coffee can and let baby pull them through a hole in the lid. If you don't have access to scarves, a piece of lightweight fabric cut into rectangles works just as well.

802. Create an activity board for your infant by attaching simple mechanisms to a sturdy, splinter-free board. Attach things that snap, roll, click, or make noise. You can find some great things at your local hardware store. Just make sure they don't contain small parts that could come off and that they're securely attached.

803. Drums can be made from empty formula cans, coffee cans, or ice cream buckets. You can decorate them with contact paper or leave them as is. Use wooden spoons as drumsticks.

804. Socks rolled up can make a great ball for baby to practice throwing. They're soft and easily gripped by little hands.

805. Boxes are a great way to keep your baby busy. Cover them with photos and magazine cutouts, and cover with clear contact paper. Your baby will enjoy turning the box to different sides and looking at the images.

806. Use large boxes of the same size to make a tunnel for your baby to crawl through. Cut out holes for your baby to peek through and decorate the inside with markers or crayons.

807. Empty lids, such as those from shaving cream and hair spray bottles, are fun for baby. Baby enjoys clapping them together, stacking them, and putting things inside them.

808. Plastic cups, bowls, and storage containers are great toys for babies. Put your baby's rattle or another toy in an ice cream or margarine container. He will enjoy shaking it and trying to figure out how to get it out.

809. An old magazine can keep your baby busy for quite some time. Make sure you supervise, as babies like to put things in their mouths.

810. An old telephone or remote control is often very entertaining for an infant. They are amused by the buttons and often like to imitate a parent talking on the phone. Be sure to remove all cords and batteries to prevent injury.

811. An old set of keys is a great distraction for a fussy baby. Make sure they are clean and sand off any sharp edges.

812. An old computer keyboard can entertain your little one. He will love the clicking noises the keys make. Make sure that you remove any cords and check for loose keys.

813. Make an activity mat for your baby by sewing objects on an old comforter or thick blanket. Sew on some small toys or attach bright pieces of fabric in different textures with Velcro, according to your child's interests and developmental stage.

814. Stuffed animals can be converted to hand puppets by removing the stuffing.

20

Media for Your Baby— and for You

BOOKS, VIDEOS, DVDS— AND FREE MAGAZINES

815. Don't buy books with paper pages for your baby. Babies love to rip and chew them, so look for something that will withstand the wear and tear. Board books, fabric books, and vinyl books are better investments.

816. Garage sales and thrift stores are great places to pick up books and videos for pennies on the dollar. Consignment and resale shops such as Once Upon a Child also stock books.

safety tip

Keep the Christmas tree out of baby's reach by placing the in a playpen.

817. Your local library can be a great resource for not only books, but also DVDs, videos, CDs, and even toys.

818. Check to see if your library offers a summer reading program. Many times even infants can participate and earn free prizes.

819. If your child loves playing with the buttons on your television or VCR, use an acrylic panoramic frame as a shield. Frames can often be found at your dollar store (compare them to more expensive shields, which can run up to $20).

820. Library book sales are a source for inexpensive used books. Check with your own local public library to see if they have one. Visit the Book Sale Finder website to search for upcoming book sales by state. www.booksalefinder.com

821. Instead of buying videotapes or DVDs, tape your child's favorite TV programs to watch later.

822. Make your own books on tape by recording yourself reading your favorite children's books. Store the tape and book together in large gallon-sized food storage bag.

823. Pick up new or gently used books, videos, and DVDs through Amazon.com's marketplace merchants. Search for items through the Amazon website as you usually would. Click on "More Buying Choices" on the product information page for any item you view. When you click the new, used, collectible, or refurbished links, you'll see the selection of products available from Amazon Marketplace sellers.

824. Overstock.com offers new books at prices that are among the lowest on the Web. Check out their "Clearance Bin" for books and other media under $4.
www.overstock.com

825. Scholastic Books holds wonderful warehouse sales at special locations throughout the year. Most books are half price with several bargain areas where paperbacks are as low as $.50 each. Dates vary by location, and some restrictions apply.
www.teacher.scholastic.com/fairs/warehouse

826. Visit the Book Closeouts website to find children's fiction and nonfiction books at bargain prices. Click on their "Clearance" tab to find books up to 85 percent off.
www.bookcloseouts.com

827. eBay is a great source for gently used books and videos. If there is a certain theme or character your child enjoys, you can often save by buying them in lots.

828. Usborne books are educational children's books available through independent sales representatives. You can earn books and other products by hosting a party in your home. To find an Usborne representative in your area, visit their website: www.ubah.com.

829. *Baby Talk* magazine, from the same publishers as *Parenting* magazine, offers a complimentary subscription to new parents. To sign up, visit their website.
www.babytalk.com

830. For a free subscription to *American Baby* magazine, visit their website and fill out a simple form. Your first issue will be on its way within 6–8 weeks.
www.americanbaby.com

831. Best Deal Magazines and Magazine Values are great online sources for inexpensive subscriptions to some of your favorite parenting magazines. Some are as little as $4 for a full year subscription.

www.bestdealmagazines.com

www.magazinevalues.com

21

Entertainment and Education

FROM THE CIRCUS TO THE LIBRARY

832. Check with your community education department to see if they offer any early childhood/infant classes. Not only are community education classes a great way to learn about your child's developmental stages, they are a great way to connect with other parents. Also, most offer low-cost or free classes to families who demonstrate financial need.

833. Call your local library to see what programs they offer for children. In addition to story hours, many libraries offer reading programs where kids can earn books and other prizes. Many are available to infants as well as older kids.

safety tip

Avoid baby reaching up for handles of pots and pans—turn them inward while cooking.

Keep all knives and other sharp utensils in latched drawers out of your child's reach.

834. Check with bookstores in your area to see if they offer programs for children. Many of them offer story hours as well as other activities for children.

835. Gymboree offers a series of parent/child programs devoted to the physical, emotional, and social development of children from infant up to age four. Visit Gymboree's website to print a coupon for a free Play and Music class at www.gymboree.com (click on "Play, Music, & Art Classes").

836. If your child registers for a Gymboree class, be sure to do it during their Gymbuck earning period. In doing so, you'll receive a voucher good for $25 off a $50 purchase at their clothing stores.

837. Sign up to receive a free circus ticket for your child from Ringling Brothers Barnum & Bailey Circus. Sign up before he turns one, and redeem the ticket later on when he is old enough to appreciate the circus. There is no expiration date. Visit www.ringling.com and click on "Special Offers."

838. Join a playgroup. A playgroup can provide companionship to both you and your child absolutely free of charge. To find one in your area visit the Matching Moms website: www.matchingmoms.com.

839. Investigate a membership at your local YMCA. Many offer swimming classes for babies as young as six months of age. They also offer free or discounted babysitting for parents who use their facilities. You may even be able to get a free membership by teaching a class, helping out at the membership desk, babysitting at their child care center, or simply by demonstrating financial need.

840. The International MOMS Club (Mothers Offering Mothers Support) caters specifically to at-home moms, whether first-timers or experienced, helping them connect with other women going through similar experiences. Membership is typically $15–$30 per year, but fees are waived for those with financial need. www.momsclub.org

841. MOPS (Mothers of Preschoolers) International is a nondenominational Christian group that supports the spiritual needs of mothers. Meetings include a guest speaker and craft project for the moms while their preschool children participate in age-appropriate activities supervised by a caregiver. The cost is typically $5 per meeting, but scholarships are available. www.gospelcom.net/mops

Part Eight:

Money—Keeping More and Spending Less

22

Family Finances

A LITTLE BIT GOES A LONG WAY

842. Apply for a social security number for your baby as soon as possible. You will need it when you file your taxes in order to claim your child as a dependent.

843. Don't forget to take advantage of the Child Tax Credit on your income tax return. Consult your tax professional to see if you qualify for other tax credits and deductions as well. Parents adopting children often qualify for additional credits.

844. Take advantage of compound interest and save as much as possible for your child early on. A $1,000 investment at age one with a 10 percent return will grow to nearly half a million dollars by the time your child reaches retirement age.

845. Make sure your family finances are in order and enlist the help of qualified professionals. Let qualified tax advisors, investment professionals, and insurance brokers help you in your family financial planning.

846. Invest in a computer program that allows you to track your spending. Quicken and Microsoft Money are both good choices.

847. A custodial account is a savings account in your child's name over which you have control until he reaches legal adulthood. The benefit of opening up a savings account in your child's name is that the first $750 of interest is tax-free. The second $750 is taxed at your child's rate, which is almost always lower than your own tax rate.

848. Switch to a 15-year mortgage if you can afford to do so. Since a significant portion of your income goes to cover your mortgage expense, owning your home outright by the time your child enters college frees up those funds to be used on education.

849. Consider a Section 529 college savings plan for your child. It allows parents to set aside money for their child's education and let it grow tax-free. The federal government won't tax your money when you take it out of the account as long as it's used for qualified education expenses. Oftentimes, you can start with as little as $25.
www.collegesavings.org

850. A Coverdell Education Savings Account allows parents to contribute up to $2,000 per year towards their child's education. No taxes are ever due on the withdrawals as long as they are used for qualified education expenses. Unlike the 529 plan, Coverdell accounts may be used for qualifying K–12 expenses.

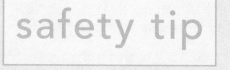

safety tip

While the risk may be minimal, your child may be exposed to dangerous bacteria after visiting a petting zoo, farm, or fair. Bacteria like E. coli and cryptosporidium can cause fever, diarrhea, and vomiting that can last up to a week. Make sure you wash your hands and your child's hands frequently, and keep hands away from baby's face and mouth. For added protection, bring along an antiseptic hand gel.

851. Roth IRA accounts can be used to save money for college. When you open up a Roth IRA, your contributions aren't tax-deductible, but they grow tax-free until they're withdrawn. If you wait the required five-year period before making a withdrawal and use them for qualified higher education expenses, your earnings are tax-free.

852. Sign up for a Upromise account and earn money for college buying the things you would normally buy. Just use a registered credit card to make your purchases at Upromise merchants. Or, earn even more by using a Upromise credit card. To sign up for free, visit their website: www.upromise.com.

853. A painless way of saving money for your child's college fund is to collect all your spare change in a large jar or piggy bank. At the end of each year or on your child's birthday, take the money to the bank and deposit it in your child's savings account. You will be surprised how quickly all of that change adds up!

854. Don't use life insurance as an invest-ment for your child. Other forms of investments provide a much higher rate of return. The main consideration of life insurance on a child should be to guarantee future insurability, not replace income.

855. Consolidate any credit card debt into a single, low-rate card. Make it your goal to pay your balance off every month if you're not doing so already.

23

Work, Hire a Sitter, or Something In-Between?

CHILD CARE

856. Join or start a babysitting co-op and trade babysitting hours with your friends. Not only do you get child care without money changing hands, you're leaving your child in the care of someone you know well and who has experience with young children.

857. Take advantage of relatives who offer to watch your kids. Not only do you get a break, your kids are creating a special bond with family members close to them.

safety tip

Never hold your baby while cooking with heat or holding hot liquids such as coffee.

858. If you have a college or university close to you, post an ad for a babysitter on its bulletin board or through its employment service. Elementary education students are looking for experience with children and opportunities to make a little money.

859. Barter for babysitting. College students may be interested in using your washing machine, borrowing your DVDs, or getting some free meals, while your neighbor may trade for lawn care or pet sitting.

860. Day care centers and family child care are less costly than an in-home provider. Some even offer financial aid for those who qualify.

861. If your employer offers a flexible spending plan, allocate a portion of your earnings towards child care. These earnings are taken out pre-tax, which, depending on your tax rate, can give you a 20 to 30 percent discount on child care.

862. Be prompt when picking up your child from a daycare center. Some child care providers charge up to $1 for every minute you're late. Coordinate your schedule with your partner so your child can be dropped off later or picked up earlier. Account for traffic and other delays when arranging a time to pick up your child.

863. Some places may allow you to help out with cleaning or making snacks or meals in exchange for a discount. It doesn't hurt to ask.

864. Split the cost of a nanny or babysitter with friends or neighbors who have children.

865. Through the Au Pair program, qualified foreign nationals live with a host family and provide child care services for up to a year while also taking classes at a post-secondary school. In return, the host family helps with the Au Pair's education expenses. For more information on the Au Pair program, visit the U.S. Department of State's website.
www.exchanges.state.gov/education/jexchanges/private/aupair.htm

STAYING HOME

866. After computing the cost of day care and expenses related to working full time, you may discover you're not making as much money as you think. Run the numbers to make a well-informed decision about staying home with your child.

867. Besides day care, you will also be saving money on transportation, work apparel, dry cleaning, and lunches out if you stay home with your child. Be sure to think of every work-related expense you will be saving and include it in your calculation.

868. Don't forget that you will be saving money on taxes if you stay home. Since most second incomes push families into a higher tax bracket, your first income will most likely be taxed at a lower rate.

869. Refinancing your home may give you a little extra cash left over at the end of the month. To calculate whether or not it is wise for your situation, visit www.money.com and run the numbers through the refinancing calculator.

870. Downgrade or give up one vehicle if you won't be using it to drive to work, or raise the deductible on your auto insurance. It may be possible for you and your spouse to share a vehicle if you're staying home with your children.

24

Clipping Coupons, Saving Money

COUPON BASICS

871. Know when *not* to use coupons. You will need to become coupon-savvy in order to recognize when coupons are a good deal and when they're not. Coupons work best when they're combined with another deal or are doubled. Carry a small calculator in your purse to help you calculate the price per unit when you're shopping.

872. Check the price on generics first. In most cases, the generic version of what you're buying is cheaper than the more expensive counterpart, even *with* a coupon.

873. Combine coupons with in-store sales and two-for-ones. A lot of grocery stores also offer "in-store" coupons. Use your own coupons in addition to these to save even more.

874. Find a store that will double your coupons. If your town doesn't have one, it may be worth a short drive to a store in another town that does. An Internet search using the key words "double, coupons + [your state]" should yield a list of stores in your area that double coupons.

875. See if your supermarket has a limit on the value of coupons it will double (for example, most double coupons up to $1.00). If so, a $1.00 coupon is worth more than a $1.50 coupon.

876. Buy the smallest size. Most people are under the impression that you will save more by buying in bulk. When using a coupon, this usually isn't true. What you will need to consider is the price per ounce. Buying a smaller size for $1.00 and getting $.50 off will yield a greater percentage savings than using the same coupon on a $2.00 item. Keep a small calculator in your purse or coupon caddy to help calculate the best deal.

877. Trade coupons with friends. Start a coupon trading group with women in your area. Let them know which items you need coupons for and offer to trade with them. To get started, email five to ten of your thrifty friends to see if they're interested. Have each friend list ten to twenty items that she always uses, and print out the lists. Keep the lists handy when you're clipping coupons, and then pass on the coupons to your friends.

878. Look for coupons in coupon bins. Some grocery stores have coupon bins within their store. Some libraries also have a coupon swapping bin. If your local library or grocer doesn't, it doesn't hurt to suggest it.

879. Find coupons online. When you think of coupons, chances are you think of the kind that come as inserts in your Sunday paper. With the popularity of the Internet, all sorts of other kinds of coupons are now available. You can download coupons from your computer and print them out.

880. Coupons are even available on eBay. Enterprising sellers are charging you for the time it takes them to clip and mail them to you. You may be able to get desirable coupons for a nominal fee.

The safest place for your baby's car seat is in the backseat. Placing it in the middle of the seat will help protect baby in the event of a side-impact collision. Be sure to use it in the rear-facing position until baby is twelve months of age.

881. Barter for coupons. Visit Mommy-saver's Bartering Board to trade coupons with other parents. www.Mommysavers.com

882. Make coupons easy to file and easy to use. A large plastic index-card box or coupon caddy from the dollar store works well. Divide your coupons by categories, such as canned goods, baby products, cereal, baking, and dairy. After serious couponing for a few months, you will discover which categories work the best for you.

883. Put your coupons for diapers, formula, and baby food in a separate envelope in your purse marked "Baby Coupons." That way, you always have them with you.

884. Always check your receipt to make sure the coupons were properly credited.

885. If you don't read the paper during the week, don't pay for the issues you're not reading. Many papers offer Sunday-only subscriptions.

886. Visit your local newspaper on Monday morning and inquire about buying leftover Sunday papers at a discount.

887. Make sure you don't cut off the portion of the coupon that lists the expiration date. Many stores won't accept them if the date is missing.

ONLINE COUPONING AND RESOURCES

888. Search for online coupon codes before making your purchase. Online retailers will frequently offer an online coupon code to encourage spending and customer loyalty. Most often they are for free shipping, 10–20 percent off your order, or $10 off a purchase of $50 or more. For a listing of current coupon codes, visit Mommysavers.com.

889. You will typically be asked to enter the code in an onscreen box some time during the checkout process. Make sure your online coupon code is reflected in your final purchase price before finalizing your order. If you fail to enter the coupon correctly, you have little recourse.

890. Make sure you're using a secure site when transferring credit card information. Look for the "https" instead of "http" in the URL to indicate you're using a secure site. Or, look for the padlock icon at the bottom of your browser.

891. Print out your receipt just in case any problems with your order should arise.

892. Visit the Cut Out Hunger website for information on which in-store sales you can combine with a coupon for the greatest savings. Their database lists stores in several states and tells you exactly how much you'll save when combining sales with a coupon. They'll even tell you the date of the circular to get the coupons needed. www.cutouthunger.org

893. Save.ca is a website for Canadian couponing. When you visit their site, you simply click on the coupons you want and they are mailed to you the next day. www.save.ca

894. Coolsavings offers printable coupons for groceries, baby products, and much more. They also feature freebies like subscriptions to *American Baby* magazine just for signing up, and membership is free. www.coolsavings.com

safety tip

To prevent burns, keep the oven door locked when it is turned on.

895. eBates offers cash back when you shop online at certain retailers, such as babyGap, JCPenney, and Barnes and Noble. Just sign up and shop through the eBates links when you make an online purchase. Signing up is free. www.ebates.com

896. Most people don't think of eBay for coupons, but this online auction site can be a great resource for avid coupon users. Bid online for the coupons you use the most. Popular coupons of interest to moms that usually pop up are for diapers and baby formula. www.ebay.com

897. Just enter your zip code on the Valu-Page website, and you can browse a weekly listing of offers available at grocery stores in your vicinity. Select the offers you want, or take them all. Print your ValuPage and take it with you on your next visit to your store. Give your Valu-Page Shopping List to the cashier to scan at the beginning of your order. www.valupage.com

898. Valpak allows you to print coupons directly from your home computer. Just enter your zip code and find coupons grouped by category. www.valpak.com

899. Eversave emails you directly with savings from local stores based on the profile you've selected. Browse available offers by state. Offers include printable coupons, samples, and freebies. www.eversave.com

900. CouponSurfer allows users to select coupons by brand name or category such as "Baby & Maternity" and "Clothing & Apparel." Print grocery coupons or browse online coupon codes. Signing up is free.
www.couponsurfer.com

901. CentsOff provides its subscribers a selection of coupons from a large database of manufacturer's coupons. Select your coupons and they are mailed directly to your home. There is a small processing fee, but if you're a regular coupon user it is worth the price.
www.centsoff.com

Part Nine:

Remembering Your Baby
for Years to Come

25

Keepsakes and Birth Announcements

KEEPSAKES

902. Purchase a scrapbook instead of a baby book. A scrapbook is usually about half the price, and it can be customized for your child. Include photos, baby's firsts, and journaling about your child.

903. Have a party! There are all sorts of scrapbooking supplies available through at-home consultants like Creative Memories, Stampin' Up, Leaving Prints, and Once Upon a Family. They can be a fun way to get some of your friends together, learn some new techniques, and earn some free merchandise. To find a representative near you, visit them online:

www.creativememories.com
www.stampinup.com
www.leavingprints.com
www.onceuponafamily.net

904. Take a photograph of your baby at the beginning of each month in the same type of clothes (such as jeans and a white T-shirt) in the same chair or next to a favorite stuffed animal.

Or, use a special vintage outfit and photograph your child in it at each birthday. It is a great way to make a side-by-side comparison of much your child has grown in relationship to something else.

905. Create a stepping stone for your garden by mixing plaster of paris in a pie plate and casting your child's handprint or footprint in it. Embellish with polished stones, mosaic tiles, seashells, or other items.

906. A handprint book is a creative way to record baby's growth. Purchase a journal or notebook with unlined paper (such as a small scrapbook). On each page, write baby's age and use an inkpad to do his handprint. Add journaling about what baby is doing at the moment and what he has recently learned.

907. An easy and inexpensive way to create a baby book with your digital photos is with MyPublisher software. Go to their website, www.mypublisher.com, and download a free copy of the software.

Click and drag your photos into their templates, then create your baby's own book adding your own titles, captions, and text. Upload your book in minutes, and you can order your custom hardbound book at a very reasonable price.

908. Make your baby's handprint in clay at home for a fraction of the cost of a prepackaged kit. Mix 1 cup baking soda, 1/2 cup cornstarch, 1 teaspoon salt, and 3/4 cup water. Heat over medium heat until boiling, then lower heat and stir until thick. Spread mixture in a mold like a whipped topping container or margarine lid. When cool, press your baby's hand into the dough to form a handprint. String with a pink or blue ribbon and use a toothpick to write the date before it dries.

909. Stores like Michaels regularly run 40 percent off coupons in their weekly circular. Use your savings to purchase high-quality scrapbooks, journals, picture frames, stickers, and calendars.

910. Sign up for the mailing list at JoAnn Fabrics & Crafts stores. In most circulars you receive, you'll get a 50 percent off coupon to use on any regular-priced item in their store.

911. Keep a baby journal to record cute sayings and jot down daily events. Both you and your child will treasure those memories as he grows older.

912. Be sure to keep the newspaper from the day your child was born. It is an inexpensive way to reflect upon what was going on in the world at that time. Add to the collection by saving a paper from each birthday, too.

913. Hate to throw out or get rid of your baby's cute infant outfits? Create a blanket made from squares of your favorite baby outfits. It is sure to be a cherished heirloom for years to come.

914. Another inexpensive keepsake is a baby's first year calendar. You can make one at home using a regular calendar or custom-make one on your computer. In each daily square, jot down a comment about your baby that day. Your comments can range from very ordinary (Nicholas loved playing peek-a-boo today) to a significant milestone (Emma took her first steps today!).

Mr. Yuck stickers are great to put on all poisonous household cleaners and medicines. Not only do they provide visual cues to young children that help them learn which items not to put in their mouth, they are often available for free from your local Poison Control Center. Find the center near you by visiting the American Association of Poison Control Centers. www.aapcc.org

915. Send a photocopy of your baby's birth certificate to the address below to receive a free congratulatory note from the president:

White House Greetings Office
Room 39
1600 Pennsylvania Avenue NW
Washington, DC 20500

916. Baby Anbesol offers a "baby tooth chart" to keep track of when baby's teeth come in. Just visit their website, print the chart, and keep it in your baby book. The chart also lists when each tooth typically erupts. www.anbesol.com

917. Bring a blank journal to your baby shower. Pass it around and ask each guest to write down his or her best parenting tips and advice.

BIRTH ANNOUNCEMENTS

918. eBay is a little-known source for birth announcements. You can frequently find beautiful announcements that are handmade to order at considerable discounts. Simply enter the search term "birth announcements" when you log on.

919. You can save a great deal by making your own baby announcements at home. Visit the Two Peas in a Bucket website for a wide range of ideas you can make yourself. www.twopeasinabucket.com

920. Purchase a onesie for your baby and use fabric paint to write his birth statistics on it. Take photos of him wearing it to use as a birth announcement. Simply address and stamp the back of the photo and sent it out as a postcard.

921. Have a photo greeting card made to announce your baby's arrival, similar to the ones families send at Christmastime. These run about $.40 each if done at a discounter. Instead of a holiday greeting, imprint with your baby's name and birth statistics.

922. If you want an elegant announcement to place in your baby book, order a more expensive announcement for immediate family and close friends only. Send an email announcement to acquaintances and others in your circle of friends. What they really want to see is a photo of your little one, not a fancy announcement.

safety tip

Place a soft, squishy mat such as a giant floor puzzle at the bottom of your stairs to cushion any falls.

923. Host a Stampin' Up party to earn products to use in making birth announcements. Stampin' Up has several stamps appropriate for baby announcements, scrapbooking, and birthday party invitations.
www.stampinup.com

924. Some websites offer great email announcements or web pages for free. They include:
www.babyzone.com
www.babiesonline.com
www.parentsplace.com

26

Recording Memories of Your Baby

TAKING PHOTOS AT HOME

925. Give your baby a piece of tape to play with while taking his or her photo. It will distract him long enough to take a few cute shots, and position his fingers where you want them.

926. Take your own portrait photos using a sheet and some props. Use simple props that don't distract from the subject: a few strands of pearl beads, a metal washtub, fresh flowers, a ball or a teddy bear, some tulle, a wagon, or antique toys all add appeal to your photos without distracting from the subject.

927. Your photos will look best with natural lighting. Position your subject in natural daylight if at all possible. When shooting outdoors, use filtered light as opposed to harsh, bright sunlight that casts blotchy shadows and makes your baby squint.

928. Don't be afraid to use generic film. Most off-brand films are made by the same manufacturer as name-brand films but are packaged differently. For example, the Kirkland brand featured at warehouse retailer Costco is made by AGFA, which is considered a high-quality film.

929. Never buy single rolls of film. Film purchased in multi-packs is much more economical. Look at warehouse stores like Sam's Club and Costco to get film in bulk.

930. Check your local warehouse clubs (Costco, Sam's Club) for their prices on film processing. Their prices are usually lower than other discount retailers.

safety tip

Make the switch from harsh chemicals to natural cleaning products such as vinegar, lemon juice, and baking soda. They are often less expensive, aren't harmful to the environment, and most important, aren't dangerous when ingested by baby. An Internet search will yield many recipes for homemade cleaners.

931. Upload your digital images to the Internet and have them shipped directly to your home. Ofoto, Snapfish, and Shutterfly frequently offer new customer promotions where you get your first set of prints developed free. These websites also allow friends and family to print or download the pictures to use themselves. www.ofoto.com www.snapfish.com www.shutterfly.com

932. Clark Color Labs and York Photo offer low-cost film developing through the mail. Just send in your roll of film with their prepaid mailer available online, and they'll send back your prints within 24 hours with another mailer to use in the future. Cost of developing a 24-exposure roll is only $1.99. www.clarkcolor.com and www.yorkphoto.com

933. Look for inexpensive picture frames at your local dollar store. Wooden ones are great because you can paint them with inexpensive craft paint to match your décor.

PROFESSIONAL PHOTOGRAPHS

934. Contact your local university or community college to see if they offer a photography major and can put you in touch with a student who would be willing to photograph your child.

935. Keep notes on certain poses, backgrounds, or props you like. Most discount portrait studios can duplicate what you like fairly well. Most studios will supply the props for you, but a teddy bear or special stuffed animal brought from home may add a special sentiment to your photograph.

936. Schedule your child's photograph for a time when he's well rested and typically in a good mood. Wait until you're at the studio to get him dressed, and bring along an extra change of clothes just in case you need them. If your child is prone to drooling, make sure he wears a bib until the last second to avoid a wet neckline.

937. Your success at a discount photography studio often depends on who is taking the photos. Ask your friends with kids if they can recommend a specific photographer and schedule your appointment with him or her.

938. If you plan on having your child's photograph taken a lot in his first year, consider buying a Smile Savers card from the Sears Portrait Studio. The initial investment is $30, but it is good for two years and pays for itself after only three sittings.

Be sure to baby proof your hotel room when traveling with baby. Bring along items like outlet covers, doorknob covers, and toilet seat latches. Get down on your hands and knees when you arrive to look for stray items the cleaning staff may have missed that baby could put in his mouth.

939. Never buy a photo from Sears without a coupon. The best deal is their one-pose portrait package special in which you get dozens of different sizes of photos for one low price. The catch is that you only get to choose one photo to create your package from.
www.searsportrait.com

940. Wal-Mart frequently advertises photo packages for less than $5, sometimes as little as $1.88. The key is to say no to the additional poses they're required to take and buy the package only.

941. The advantage of having your child's portrait done at Picture People is that your photos are ready in an hour, compared to other studios where you have to wait weeks. They have over 300 stores nationwide and are owned by Hallmark.
www.picturepeople.com

942. JCPenney portrait studios are also reasonable. Members of their Portrait Club pay no sitting fees and receive coupons, offers, and discounts for two years. Watch your Sunday paper and look online for additional coupons.
www.jcpportraits.com

943. Target portrait studios have no sitting fees and you select your portrait package from your favorite pose. Look in your Sunday paper and online to find photos for portrait packages under $10. Find The Studio by calling 1-888-887-8994 or visiting their website at www.target.com.

944. When you get your wallet-sized portraits back from a discount portrait studio, most come with white edges. Cut the white edges off and finish with a corner rounder. It creates a more finished appearance and gives your photos a professional look.

GOING DIGITAL

945. Contact local camera shops or newspaper photographers to see if they are interested in selling any of their cameras. Such places are always upgrading their equipment to include the most state-of-the-art camera equipment and their castoffs are usually in pretty good shape.

946. Sometimes you can find refurbished cameras at considerable savings at camera shops. Most also come with a warranty and an option for buying an extended warranty, so you don't need to be hesitant about buying one.

947. Pawn shops, rent-to-own stores, and eBay are other sources for used camera equipment.

948. The optical zoom is more important than the digital zoom. Digital zoom gives the appearance of a close-up image without the quality of optical zoom.

949. Make sure the camera you buy comes with rechargeable batteries.

950. You probably won't need any more than three or four megapixels, so don't pay for what you don't need. A four megapixel camera produces great 4 x 6 prints and enlargements up to 11 x 14 without compromising quality.

951. Consider buying a digital camera if you don't have one already. You would be amazed by the number of photographs you'll take in baby's first months. A digital camera saves money on film and allows you to delete the images that didn't turn out. Burn the photos you want to archive onto a CD for easy storage.

952. Instead of printing digital photos at home, have them printed at Wal-Mart, Sam's Club, or Costco. If you're having 4 x 6 images made, it costs more in printer ink and paper to do it at home. You can even upload your photos to their website and pick them up in-store, creating one less trip out with your infant.

CAMCORDERS

953. Springtime is a good time to purchase a camcorder. That's when the new models are introduced and older inventory is liquidated. Never purchase a camcorder that's just come onto the market. Wait a few months until its price has been reduced.

954. Purchase a digital video recorder if you can afford to do so. Just like VHS tapes, analog video is quickly becoming obsolete. Digital cameras feature better picture quality, allow you to edit your videos on your home computer, and their batteries have a longer running time. The average home user can get by with a low-to-mid-range model that costs under $500.

955. When buying a digital camcorder, look for at least a 10x optical zoom lens and image stabilization.

956. Don't pay extra for a camcorder that captures still images if you already have a digital camera. The images captured by camcorders are low-resolution compared to the images that still cameras produce. It may be convenient to carry only one camera, but you'll be disappointed with the results.

27

Special Occasions

FIRST BIRTHDAY

957. Parents can't wait to commemorate their child's first birthday with a celebration. Unlike the birthdays to come, this party is really more for you. Resist the urge to go overboard. Keep the guest list small. At this age, your child will become easily overwhelmed with a large group and experience sensory overload.

958. The focus of the first party should be on creating special memories of the event rather than on expensive decorations, food, and party favors. Invest your time in ideas that will help your celebration be fun and memorable.

959. Have a "cake and ice cream only" birthday party. Let your guests know what you'll be serving so they can eat beforehand. You'll save big by not having to make a meal for your guests.

960. Start a "birthday tablecloth" for your child. Have guests sign the tablecloth, noting their favorite memory of your child from the past year. You can also do your child's handprints on it with an inkpad. Be sure to date each entry. Over a period of time your child will have a wonderful keepsake.

961. Instead of having guests bring your baby a gift, have everyone bring an item for a time capsule that the birthday child can open when he is older. Items could be a photo of the guest with the birthday child, a current newspaper or magazine, a grocery receipt, or an advertisement.

962. Try making your baby's cake yourself. An Internet search will yield dozens of sites with specific instructions on how to make the cake of your choice.

safety tip

When selecting toys for car trips, be sure to choose soft toys such as plush animals and fabric books. Any unrestrained item poses a threat that could lead to injury when in a car crash. Make sure you place shopping bags and other cargo in the trunk or behind the backseat in an SUV or minivan whenever possible. Smaller items can be stored under a seat or in the glove compartment.

963. Check with your local supermarkets to see if they offer a free first birthday cake for your child. Many offer a free sheet cake or small cake for baby if a larger one is purchased.

964. Look at the dollar store for decorations. You will often find liquidated merchandise from more expensive party stores there. Oftentimes you can find the same themes and characters you're after.

965. Mylar helium balloons, which can run up to $5 at party stores, can often be found at the dollar store. Mylar balloons can also be saved and refilled with helium when you want to use them again.

966. Instead of more toys, ask relatives who will be giving gifts to make a contribution to your child's savings account. Take advantage of the fact your child doesn't realize it is his or her birthday. At this age, your child won't miss out on anything. By age two or three he will come to expect more in the way of gifts.

967. Plant a tree on your baby's first birthday. Take a picture of him next to the tree each year to record his growth along with the tree's growth.

968. Start a birthday scrapbook. Include photos of the birthday child and his guests, the cake, and decorations. Have each guest sign the book along with a favorite memory of the birthday child. Include a copy of the invitation and jot some notes about what you did and what gifts your child received.

969. Receive a First Birthday card from the White House by sending your baby's name, address, and birth date on a postcard to:

White House Greetings Office
Room 39
1600 Pennsylvania Avenue NW
Washington, DC 20500

BAPTISM

970. Most department stores carry baptismal gowns and suits for babies, which typically run $40–$75 on up. Be sure to check off-price retailers that stock many of the same items as department stores, such as Ross, Marshalls, TJ Maxx, and even Wal-Mart. You may find the same thing at considerable savings.

971. If you sew, make your baby's baptism gown out of your wedding dress train. It is a special way to reuse something that was very meaningful to you at one time, and leaves your dress intact if you want to pass it on to a daughter someday.

CHRISTMAS

972. Each year at Christmastime, buy a charm to sew onto your baby's stocking. The first year may be a baby bottle, rattle, or teddy bear. Each year you can add to the collection by adding a charm that has something to do with your child's year.

973. Use extra wallet photos or snapshots of your child as gift tags. Just punch a hole in the corner, and write to and from on the back.

974. It is hard to resist buying a Baby's First Christmas ornament for your child. However, if you wait until after Christmas to buy it, you can save up to 75 percent or more. You will still have it in years to come to remember the first Christmas by.

975. Start the tradition of making an ornament for each child at Christmastime. Write your child's name and the year on the ornament as a lasting keepsake.

976. Don't spend your money on photos of your child with Santa at the mall. Most are poor quality and quite expensive. If you ask, many Santas will allow you to take a snapshot with your own camera.

HALLOWEEN

977. Search for costumes on eBay. Begin your search early enough to allow sufficient time for shipping.

978. Thrift stores are great places to find either complete costumes or to look for pieces to assemble one of your own.

979. Costumes can be made at home with hooded sweat suits, sleepers, or other items you may have in your home already. Many of them require no sewing and very little time.

safety tip

Never have your baby or toddler wear a mask as part of his Halloween costume. If your child finds it difficult to breath with the mask on, he will not be able to tell you. Instead, use nontoxic face paint to create a special look. If your child has sensitive skin, skip the face paint altogether.

980. **Dalmatian.** For an inexpensive Dalmatian costume, buy a white hooded sweat suit and adhere spots using black felt and glue. Cut the spots accordingly, and adhere with tacky glue. Since the glue is washable, you can peel off the spots when you're done and use the suit again. Cut ears and pin on the hood with a safety pin. Add a black nose with a little makeup.

981. **Mouse.** To make a mouse costume, start with a hooded gray sweatshirt and sweatpants. Make ears out of gray and pink felt, then sew or pin onto the hood. Take a gray tube sock and fill with newspaper or fiberfill to make a tail. Paint on a pink nose with a little lipstick and draw whiskers on with a little black eyeliner.

982. **Ghost.** For small children under three feet tall, take a white pillowcase and cut holes for the eyes and arms. Have them wear a white long-sleeved shirt underneath, and you have a cute ghost costume.

983. **Ladybug**. For this costume, you'll need a black shirt and leggings, pipe cleaners, small pom-poms, and two pieces of red felt. Using a plate, trace a large circle on the felt and paint black dots on it using a permanent marker or black fabric paint. Cut the felt in half for the wings and attach to the back of your child's shirt with safety pins. The antennae are made with black pipe cleaners attached to a headband (add 2 pom-poms on the end).

984. **Peas in a Pod**. If you have multiples, convert your double stroller into a peapod by covering it with a green sheet (take an old white sheet and dye with fabric dye). Cut out a strip long enough to reveal your twins (or triplets!) dressed in green sleepers.

985. **Bumblebee**. Use tacky glue to adhere 1 1/2 inch black strips of felt to a yellow onesie, sleeper, or shirt. Use pipe cleaners attached to a headband for antennae, and hot-glue a pom-pom to each end.

986. **Flower**. Create a flower costume with a green sweat suit and bunch of artificial flowers purchased at your dollar store or discount outlet. Cut the flowers apart and hot-glue them to a hat, and glue the leaves to the collar of the sweat suit.

987. **Chicken**. Pair a white turtleneck with yellow tights for a cute chicken costume. Add white feathers from a boa and use yellow kitchen gloves for the feet and hands. The chicken's head can be made from a white cap adding red felt as the comb to the part that ties under the chin.

988. **Pumpkin**. Starting with an orange sweat suit (use fabric dye if you can't find one), add black felt for the triangle jack-o'-lantern face on your child's torso. A green hat can be used for the stem, adding some artificial leaves with tacky glue.

989. **Skunk**. This costume can be made in minutes by dressing your child in a black hooded sweat suit. Add black gloves, stuff a small black sock for the tail, and add masking tape down the back for the skunk's stripe.

990. **Scarecrow**. A simple flannel shirt and overalls can be transformed into an adorable scarecrow costume. Add a little straw peeking out of the sleeves, add flannel patches to the overalls with tacky glue, and have your child wear a straw hat. Look for a decorative bird in the artificial floral department to add to the hat.

991. **Black Cat**. Similar to the skunk costume, this uses a black sweat suit. Add black gloves, stuff one side of a pair of black tights for the tail, and add ears to the hood with black felt. Eyeliner can be used to draw a nose and whiskers on your child's cheeks.

EASTER

992. After-Easter sales are a good time to stock up on dressy apparel for your child. Try to anticipate what lightweight coats, shoes, dresses, and suits he or she will need for the coming year and buy ahead.

993. You can often find cute stuffed animals on clearance after Easter for 50 to 75 percent off. It's a great time to purchase stocking stuffers or party favors for the year ahead.

TIPS FOR TRAVELING WITH BABY

994. A cooler can double as a baby bathtub. Make sure that all soapy water has been cleaned out after you're done using it.

995. Carry a small elastic belt with you in your diaper bag. In a restaurant, it can be used to secure baby in a high chair with a broken strap. It can be used to keep your child safely seated in a shopping cart as well.

996. When you travel with an older baby who may be eating snacks in a car seat, be sure to put down a sheet on the floor of your vehicle. It will make cleanup much easier and preserve the interior of your car.

997. Children under two fly free if you carry them on your lap. To keep baby restrained while in flight, consider wearing a front-pack or baby carrier.

998. Look for flights that aren't full to increase your odds of getting an empty seat next to you for your infant. Monday afternoon through Thursday morning flights are typically considered off-peak and planes are less likely to be completely booked. You're also more likely to get a deal on your tickets if you're flying off-peak.

999. In most cases, you can reserve your seat assignment online before you arrive at the airport. Try to book a seat with an empty one next to it. Or, arrive at the airport early to request special seating if available.

1000. If you do book a seat for your child, be sure to enroll him or her in a frequent flier program. Even infants can earn miles towards free flights.

Index

C

About the Author

Kimberly Danger holds a degree in marketing from Minnesota State University, Mankato. She is the owner and creator of Mommysavers.com, an online resource for parents interested in saving time and money. Kimberly lives in southern Minnesota with her husband and two kids. Her hobbies include reading, scrapbooking, photography, and, of course, finding bargains.

NOTES

NOTES

NOTES

NOTES

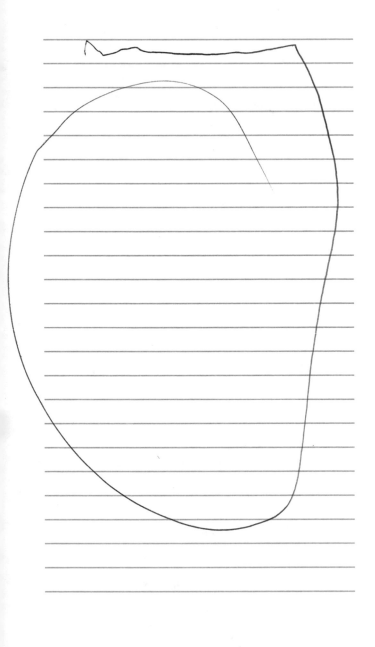